PENRHYN CASTLE

Gwynedd

ÆQUO · ANIMO

THE NATIONAL TRUST

This guidebook draws on the work of many people who have researched aspects of the Penrhyn story, in particular the late Brigadier A. P. Trevor of Beaumaris, who generously shared with the National Trust the results of his research, and whose notes are on deposit at University College, North Wales, Bangor. Mr E. H. Douglas Pennant has advised the Trust on matters of genealogy and has written the bulk of the chapters on family history, in collaboration with Mr Tomos Roberts, archivist at UCNW, who has been unfailingly helpful in allowing access to the family papers in his care. To Mr Douglas Pennant, and his parents Mr J. C. and Lady Janet Douglas Pennant, who instigated the conveyance of Penrhyn Castle and 40,000 acres of land to the Trust in 1951, we are continually grateful.

The Appendix has been written by Dr Tim Mowl, whose doctoral thesis on the Norman Revival has been of great assistance in preparing other parts of this book. Chapters Two, Three, Six and Eight are by Jonathan Marsden, formerly Historic Buildings Representative for North Wales; Chapter Five and the individual picture entries by Alastair Laing, the Trust's Pictures Curator; Chapter Seven by A. W. Lord, formerly Gardens Adviser. Extracts from Queen Victoria's journals are reproduced by gracious permission of Her Majesty the Queen, and from the journal of Lord Hatherton of Teddesley by permission of the Staffordshire Record Office.

For help in various ways the Trust is grateful to Pamela Clark, P. R. Coltson, Ann Datta, C. J. Dawkins, Tim Egan, John Hardy, Mark Hickman, Jana Horak, Frances Lynch, Gill Medland, Lady Millar, Anthony Ratcliffe, Dr Aileen Ribeiro, Neil Stratford, the Lord Sudeley, Stephen Somerville, Clive Wainwright, Stephen Winsor and Lucy Wood.

First published in Great Britain in 1991 by the National Trust

© 1991 The National Trust
Registered charity no. 205846
Reprinted 1993, 1999, 2002, 2006, 2007; revised 1994, 1997, 2001, 2004

ISBN 978-1-84359-116-0

Photographs: Aerofilms page 22; A. C. Cooper page 10; *Country Life* pages 21 (bottom), 50, 78, 80 (bottom), 82; Gwynedd Archives page 80 (top); Angelo Hornak pages 20 (top), 31 (bottom); Christopher Hurst page 8 (top right); Jean Lindsay page 87; John Mills pages 12, 30, 32, 34 (top right), 37, 38, 39, 60, 67, 83; The National Library of Wales page 13 (top and bottom); Trustees of the National Gallery, London page 34 (bottom); National Portrait Gallery, London page 20 (bottom); National Trust Photographic Library/Mike Caldwell pages 28 (bottom), 44, 45 (top), 47, 48, 49, 52, 53, (top), 54, 59, 62, back cover; NTPL/Andreas von Einsiedel pages 53 (bottom), 56, 63; NTPL/Matthew Antrobus front cover; NTPL/John Hammond pages 67, 68 (top and bottom), 69; NT/Robert O. Eames pages 14 (top), 23, 24 (top left), 26 (top left), 75, 81, 84; NT/Kevin Richardson page 4; Royal Photographic Society, Bath page 86; H. Tempest (Cardiff) Ltd page 88.

Designed by James Shurmer

Phototypeset in Monotype Bembo Series 270
by Intraspan Ltd, Smallfield, Surrey (is314)

Printed by BAS
for National Trust (Enterprises) Ltd,
Heelis, Kemble Drive, Swindon, Wilts SN2 2NA

CONTENTS

CHAPTER ONE

THE EARLY OWNERS OF PENRHYN

The society of thirteenth-century North Wales had changed little for centuries. It was a world of rural communities of free and bondmen with few large settlements, subject to the personal rule of the local Welsh prince and liable to be disrupted by periodic invasion from England. During the thirteenth century land settlement and ownership gradually became more defined and the prizes for those who successfully acquired land could be vast.

Men in the political service of the Princes of Gwynedd at that time could expect to be rewarded with large tracts of land, free from any due or service. The most notable examples of such rewarding must be the cases of Ednyfed Fychan (d.1246), seneschal (or steward) to the prince, Llywelyn ab Iorwerth, and his sons Goronwy ab Ednyfed (d.1268) and Tudur ab Ednyfed (d.1278). These three men were rewarded with large areas of land in many parts of North Wales and as far south as Dyfed.

Part of the lands given to Goronwy ab Ednyfed was a promontory containing over 500 acres of land, immediately east of Bangor, which has been known for centuries as *Penrhyn* (literally meaning 'promontory'). Officially, it was known as *Gafael Goronwy ab Ednyfed*, 'the holding of Goronwy ab Ednyfed'. The holding passed to Goronwy's descendants and their families who grew independent of each other until the late fourteenth century when Gwilym ap Gruffydd married Morfudd, daughter of Goronwy Fychan of Penmynydd, Anglesey, who held the other share of Gafael Goronwy ab Ednyfed. Thus Gwilym was able to reunite Gafael Goronwy ab Ednyfed, which became the centre of the estate he was to build – the first large landed estate in North Wales.

(Left) The rugged landscape of Snowdonia on the Penrhyn estate, with the snow-capped Tryfan in the background

Political events, however, were to intervene. In September 1400 Owain Glyndŵr was proclaimed Prince of Wales and entered into open rebellion against the English crown. The uncles of Gwilym ap Gruffydd's wife, Morfudd, were close relatives of Owain Glyndŵr and were amongst his staunchest supporters. Gwilym himself held aloof for some time, but joined the rebellion in 1402. In 1406 he surrendered to the English king, Henry IV, and the following year his lands became forfeit to the crown because of his part in the rebellion. Yet within eight months he had succeeded in buying back his own lands. Later he was also able to purchase those of his relatives forfeited during the rebellion. During this period Morfudd died and Gwilym then married Joan Stanley, daughter of Sir William Stanley of Hooton, Cheshire. This was a crucial marriage which established a close connection that was to last for over a century with the Stanley family, who were already powerful landowners in the North West.

From about 1410 Gwilym's estate began to grow rapidly. He bought lands systematically in the parish of Llandygai and on Anglesey, and Gafael Goronwy ab Ednyfed, now known as Penrhyn, became the demesne land of the estate, farmed directly by him. At some time between 1410 and his death in 1431 Gwilym built a fortified manor house with its own tower at Penrhyn, on land belonging to his mother Generys, according to a note in the hand of Gwilym's son, William, on the back of a legal document – a very rare example of such evidence.[1] The house and its adjacent chapel stood more or less intact until about 1786. A poem by the fifteenth-century Welsh poet Rhys Goch Eryri compares Gwilym's tower with the Eagle Tower of Caernarfon Castle and states that the work on Gwilym's tower is finer. He describes the whitewashed manor house as standing between Menai and the mountains

A fragment of the medieval chapel built by Gwilym ap Gruffydd, which was re-erected to the north west of the house in the late eighteenth century

and also mentions the chapel (which still stands). Rhys ends his poem with an even bolder comparison: 'If one dared ... to compare the Court of God on high ... with an earthly court. The appearance of Gwilym's court ... is more like ... the cloister of God than the court of man'.[2]

Gwilym died in 1431, the founder of an estate based on inheritance, marriage, purchase, enterprise and political wisdom. He was succeeded at Penrhyn by his son from his second marriage, who became known as William Griffith or Gwilym Fychan. In 1443 he was released from the restrictions of the penal laws that Henry IV had imposed on Welshmen following the suppression of Owain Glyndŵr's rebellion, on the condition that he married an Englishwoman and held no public office. In 1447 he married Alice Dalton of Apethorpe, Northamptonshire, who had Stanley family connections. Throughout William's life the Penrhyn estate continued to grow, mostly now by purchase. Like his father, he bought lands in Bangor, Llandygai and Anglesey and towards the end of his life turned his attention to the Llŷn Peninsula. By his death at Plas Newydd on Anglesey in 1483, almost the whole of the parish of Llandygai was part of the Penrhyn estate.

He was succeeded in 1483 by his son, also called William Griffith. He was appointed Chamberlain of North Wales by Richard III in 1483 and married Joan Troutbeck, a niece of Sir Thomas Stanley, later to become the 1st Earl of Derby. Just before the defeat and death of Richard III at Bosworth in 1485, William Griffith was dragged into the vortex of a political storm, probably because of his connections with the Stanley family. It had become obvious to Richard that Sir Thomas Stanley held the military balance in England and in order to secure his allegiance he imprisoned his son, George Stanley, Lord Strange, in Nottingham Castle, together with William Griffith, his kinsman. Both men survived and their families flourished under the new king, the Welshman Henry VII. William Griffith was made a Knight Bachelor in 1489 and remained Chamberlain until his death in 1505–6.

Sir William Griffith was succeeded by his son, also called William Griffith. The third William Griffith was an Esquire of the Body of the King in 1509 and was appointed Chamberlain of North Wales in the same year. One of his fellow esquires was Charles Brandon, later to become Duke of Suffolk. William Griffith subsequently served under Brandon during the English expedition against France in 1513, and was knighted in the field at Tournai.

On Sir William's death in 1531 the Penrhyn estate passed to his son, Edward, a professional soldier who saw service in Ireland. In 1540 he died of dysentry in Dublin Castle, leaving a wife, Jane Puleston, three young daughters, Jane, Catherine and Ellen, and a brother, Rhys Griffith. Following his death disputes arose as to his true heirs which led to court action. After two years the court made an award which, in effect, was to split up the medieval Penrhyn estate. Most of the Anglesey lands were to be divided between Edward Griffith's three daughters, while the Caernarfonshire lands, including Penrhyn, were to go to Rhys Griffith. Decades of litigation followed.

Rhys Griffith, who was knighted in 1547, died in 1580, and was succeeded by the eldest son of his third marriage, Pyrs Griffith, then a minor aged 12. Pyrs Griffith is perhaps the most enigmatic and interesting member of the Griffith family. There are many legends concerning him. He is said to have been a pirate or a privateer; to have taken part in the campaign against the Armada in 1588 and to have had a secret tunnel built from Abercegin (later Port Penrhyn) to Penrhyn Castle. There is a certain amount of documentary evidence to support the legends. He was a poet and all his surviving Welsh poems concern the sea. He did capture a Spanish ship, the *Speranza* of Ayamonte in 1600 and brought it to Abercegin with a cargo of olive oil, earthernware and silk. In 1603 he was arrested on board his ship in Cork harbour by a Captain Charles Plessington, who described him as 'Captain Pierce Griffith, a notable pirate'; little remained of his cargo but oils, rotten ginger and logwood.

Pyrs Griffith had not come into his inheritance until 1591. He mortgaged the first part of the Penrhyn estate in 1592. There followed mortgage after mortgage until 1616. During this period he was also involved in much litigation concerning encroachments and illegal possession of his lands, suggesting that he spent much time at sea and was not in a position to supervise his estate. A fellow poet, seafarer and landowner, Thomas Prys of Plas Iolyn (?1564–1634) wrote several poems to Pyrs Griffith. In one he sends a porpoise from the Menai Strait to Spanish waters to bring Pyrs Griffith back to his home and his lands:

> May God of his grace give him as a treasure
> Grace to depart from the sea[3]

In 1616 his father-in-law, Sir Thomas Mostyn, had Pyrs Griffith put in the Fleet prison in London for non-payment of monies due under his marriage settlement. In the following year the Penrhyn estate finally passed to Ievan Lloyd of Iâl, to whom large parts of it had already been mortgaged. Thus the connection between the Griffith family and Penrhyn came to an end. Pyrs died in 1628 and was buried in Westminster Abbey.

In 1622 Ievan Lloyd sold the Penrhyn estate to John Williams, a descendant of Robin ap Gruffydd, Gwilym ap Gruffydd's brother, and thus a distant kinsman of Pyrs Griffith. John Williams's purchase reunited Penrhyn with the neighbouring Cochwillan estate, for the hall-house at Cochwillan had been built by Gwilym ap Gruffydd's great-nephew

John Williams, Archbishop of York (1582–1650), who acquired the Penrhyn estate in 1622

and namesake between 1452 and 1480. The house and estate at Cochwillan passed down through the family, which took the name of Williams. After 1612 they passed from Henry Williams and his family to the Earl of Pembroke and his family, which sold them to John Williams in 1622.

John Williams (1582–1650) was successively Dean of Salisbury and of Westminster, Lord Keeper of the Great Seal, Bishop of Lincoln and Archbishop of York. Thomas Pennant, the celebrated naturalist and topographer, and distant relative of the Pennants of Penrhyn, gives a full and unflattering account of his life, considering him '. . . as a wise but not as a good man. . . a great minister but a bad divine'.[4] When a child at Conwy he would play at leaping from the medieval town walls to the shore; and on one occasion 'the fall was on so critical a part,' wrote Pennant, 'as ever to secure him from all reproaches of unchastity'.[5] Educated at Ruthin School and St John's College, Cambridge, he was appointed Lord Keeper of the Great Seal in 1621. At the start of the Civil War in 1642 he was entrusted by the King with the defence of Conwy. Ousted from the command of Conwy in 1645, he promptly offered his services to the Parliamentarian Sir John Mytton in laying siege to the castle. The news of the

King's execution affected him deeply and he died at Gloddaeth, near Conwy, in 1650. His kneeling effigy in Llandygai church is accompanied by a helm and spurs. On his death the Penrhyn estate (as the two estates will be referred to henceforth) passed to his nephew, Griffith Williams. Emulating his uncle, Griffith Williams served at different times the Commonwealth, the Protectorate and (after 1660) the King. In 1658 he became one of the thirteen baronets created by Cromwell. The honour was annulled at the Restoration, but recreated by Charles II in 1661.

Griffith Williams died in 1663 and was succeeded by his eldest son, Sir Robert Williams, 2nd Baronet, who married a daughter of Sir John Glynne, an

Sir Griffith Williams, 1st Baronet (d. 1663)

ambitious lawyer of Hawarden in Flintshire, who, like Griffith Williams, served first the Parliamentarian and then the royalist cause with equal success. Glynne imposed such a severe marriage settlement on his son-in-law that the couple were forced to leave Penrhyn and live in Chester. In 1680 Sir Robert was succeeded by his elder son, Sir John Williams, 3rd Baronet, who died without issue two years later. His brother, Sir Griffith, 4th Baronet, fared no better and died in 1684. At this point the title and estate went separate ways, the title passing to Sir Robert Williams's brother, Hugh.

The estate remained effectively intact throughout the first half of the eighteenth century, but ownership became increasingly fragmented among the 2nd Baronet's descendants. In 1767 Anne, Lady Yonge sold her portion to John and Henry Pennant, sons of Edward Pennant of Clarendon, Jamaica.

The Pennants stemmed from Flintshire, where in the 1480s their ancestor Thomas Pennant had rebuilt Basingwerk Abbey while its abbot. The abbot's great-grandson, Gifford, or Giffard, Pennant, a

The tomb of John Williams in Llandygai church

captain in the Horse, emigrated to Jamaica in 1658 and established sugar plantations in the parish of Clarendon.

The Pennants were pioneers in developing what was to become a vastly profitable industry. Sugar cane was introduced to Jamaica from Brazil by the Dutch in the 1640s. Following the final expulsion of the Spanish from Jamaica in 1660, English settlers such as the Pennants were free to concentrate on satisfying the growing European preference for sugar as a sweetener for food and in particular the newly fashionable hot drinks, tea and coffee. The success of the planters' estates depended on a large labour force of slaves, which was supplied by the Triangular Trade. Manufactured goods were exported from Britain to West Africa with which to buy slaves. The slaves were transported from there on the dreaded 'middle passage' to the West Indies, where they were employed to cut and gather the sugar canes. These were brought to the mills by ox-carts and crushed in rollers pulled by mules or cattle, but later powered by steam. Nearby, the mashed liquor was poured into coppers for boiling and progressively reduced until it could be left to crystallise while the molasses that ran off during

cooling was converted into rum. Quicklime was added at the boiling stage as a preservative and an aid to crystallisation. The crystallised sugar and its by-products, rum and molasses, were returned to Britain in the third leg of the trade. By the mid-eighteenth century the West Indies were the most valuable part of the British Empire and the wealth of the Jamaican planters had become proverbial.[6]

Gifford Pennant's son Edward (1672–1736) extended the family estates further, becoming Chief Justice of Jamaica and a member of the governing Council. Edward Pennant's neighbours on the island at this time included Peter Beckford, a cousin and ancestor of the celebrated creator of Fonthill, and Henry Dawkins, grandfather of the builder of Penrhyn Castle.

Edward divided his estates between his sons John, Samuel and Henry Pennant. The ambition of most planters was to escape the disease and uncertain climate of the West Indies and become absentee landlords, leaving the chore of managing their estates to attorneys or foremen. Edward Pennant's sons were no different. Samuel (1709–50) departed for London in 1732 and became a partner of Messrs Drake and Long, West India Merchants, thence-

Sugar-making in the late seventeenth century. The sugar canes were crushed in the sugar mill between rollers pulled by oxen. The mashed liquor was run off into coppers where it was boiled and then allowed to crystallise. From the English edition of Pierre Pomet's 'A Compleat History of Druggs' (1737)

Sir Samuel Pennant (1709–50). He left the family estates in the West Indies for a career in London, becoming Lord Mayor in 1749. (No.47, Passage to Keep)

forth Drake, Pennant and Long. He left the partnership in 1740 to become Common Councilman for the Cheap ward of London, and in 1742 he was elected Alderman for Bishopgate ward. From 1744 to 1745 he served as one of the Sheriffs of London during the second Jacobite Rebellion, and for his defence of the City and his loyalty to the Hanoverian cause, he was knighted by George II in 1745. In 1749 he became Lord Mayor, but died in office the following year as a result of a virulent strain of jail-fever, contracted while presiding as a judge, from a plaintiff who fatally infected another twenty occupants of the same courtroom before succumbing himself. Samuel Pennant's estates became the property of his brothers as 'tenants-in-common'.

John and Henry Pennant had settled in England in 1739. John became a successful merchant in Liverpool, the chief British port for the sugar trade, and in 1761 acquired his brother Henry's Jamaican property as a lifetime gift. The Pennant brothers also began acquiring property in Britain, gradually

reuniting the divided Penrhyn estate in their own hands. In 1765 John Pennant's only surviving son and heir, Richard Pennant (1739–1808), married the heiress to one portion of the Penrhyn estate, Anne Susannah Warburton. Two years later the brothers bought Anne, Lady Yonge's portion and in 1768 John was assigned the rents from that of her son, Sir George Yonge. On the death of Anne Warburton's father, General Hugh Warburton, in 1771, Richard Pennant inherited the Warburton share, which included the Penrhyn demesne, together with Winnington Hall and estate, with its lucrative salt workings, in Cheshire. When Henry died unmarried in 1772, he passed his share in Penrhyn to his brother. Thus, when John himself died in 1781, Richard Pennant was in possession of three-quarters of the estate and receiving the rents of the other quarter (Sir George Yonge's portion). In 1785 he reunited the entire estate for the first time since 1713 by purchasing the Yonge property.

NOTES

1 See *Penrhyn Further Additional MSS*, University College, North Wales, Bangor.

2 For the text and translation, see Henry Lewis *et al.*, *Cywyddau Iolo Goch ac Eraill*, Caerdydd, 1937, pp.310–13; E. H. Douglas Pennant, *The Welsh Families of Penrhyn*, 1985, p.18.

3 For the text and translation, see F. Fisher, ed., *The Cefn Coch MSS*, Liverpool, 1899, pp.112–15; E. H. Douglas Pennant, op. cit., pp.22–3.

4 *Tours in Wales*, 1810, iii, p.101.

5 Ibid., p.96.

6 See Jean Lindsay, 'The Pennants and Jamaica, 1665–1800', I and II, *Trans. Caernarvonshire Historical Society*, 1982 and 1983.

CHAPTER TWO
RICHARD PENNANT, IMPROVER

Richard Pennant (1739–1808) is one of the lesser known, but most impressive industrial and agrarian improvers of the later eighteenth century. The circumstances of his birth are obscure, as it coincided with the return of his parents, John and Bonella, from the West Indies to England; he may even have been born at sea during the voyage. He was educated at Trinity College, Cambridge, and most of his early career was spent building on his father's success as a Liverpool merchant. West Indian connections secured him the sponsorship of Alderman Beckford in entering Parliament as MP for Petersfield in Hampshire in 1761. Through the influence of his wife Anne Susannah, whose grandfather had been a Liverpool MP, he secured one of the two Liverpool seats in 1767 and held it initially until 1780, speaking often in the House, particularly on trade matters and in support of the American colonists' grievances.

When his father died in 1781, Richard had already decided on the formula for his later success, which was to apply the profits from the family's West Indian sugar plantations to the wholesale development of their Caernarfonshire estates. The effect was not to be confined to the Penrhyn lands. In fact, his succession has been called 'the crucial turning point in the economic development of Caernarvonshire ...'[1]

Though extensive, the Penrhyn estate which Richard Pennant inherited would have seemed unpromising to many. The tortuous line of succession (see Chapter One) had led to chronic under-investment, and 'the country was scarcely passable, the roads not better than very bad horse-paths, the cottages wretched, the farmers poor'.[2] Pennant's collaborators in bringing about his revolution were members of the ingenious Wyatt family of Staffordshire, which from the mid-eighteenth century produced twenty-eight architects, a President of the

Royal Academy and of the Royal Institute of British Architects, and three knights. It also produced a dynasty of outstanding land agents who served the Penrhyn estate for a hundred years from 1786.[3]

Pennant had employed the most famous Wyatt, James, in adding a wing to Winnington Hall in 1776, but at Penrhyn it was to his brother Samuel (1737–1807) that he turned to modernise the ancient hall-house he had inherited. Wyatt's designs respected the earlier structure to a large extent, though they were revised in order to relocate the stables. He retained the cellars and the spiral stair in the north-west corner, but transformed the great hall into a symmetrical entrance hall, and added turrets and crenellations and a further wing of family rooms at the south east. The house was built in a curious form of castellated Gothic, and what struck most visitors was its colour, resulting from hanging 'mathematical' tiles on the walls, which gave the appearance of yellow brick. 'Penrhyn glitters in its yellow glory', wrote a visitor in 1791, 'beautifully contrasted with the pure white of the interspersed cottages of the plain.'[4] No less remarkable was the new park gateway, which formerly stood near the site of the present home farm. It took the form of a triumphal arch, possibly – like 'Athenian' Stuart's arch at Shugborough in Staffordshire – based on the Arch of Hadrian at Rome.

In 1786 another brother, Benjamin Wyatt (1745–1818) was appointed general agent to the estate, which he remained until 1817. Though the agricultural character of his native Staffordshire was quite different, he quickly identified the main deficiencies of farming on the predominantly mountainous estate. His remedies were the provision of shelter and winter fodder. Shelter came either in the form of new buildings (which he designed himself) or from plantations. By 1800 it was estimated that 600,000 trees had been planted on the estate, and the improvement of the farmland was accelerated by drainage and manuring. Wyatt introduced turnips and scotch cabbage for fodder, and encouraged crop rotation. In 1789 all the farm leases were renewed with printed documents including clauses on correct husbandry.

It was slate that was to transform the fortunes of Richard Pennant and Penrhyn. The word 'slate' is related to the French *esclater*, meaning 'to break into pieces', for it has the unusual geological property that it can be split cleanly into thin but strong sheets of almost any size, which make an ideal roofing material. Slate is found in much of north-west Wales and had been extracted from the mountain at

Cae Braich y Cafn at the north end of the Nant Ffrancon valley since at least the fifteenth century, but the remoteness of the region and the lack of good roads meant that it had remained a largely local activity. By the 1760s quarrying was still on a very small scale, with dozens of workings being exploited by as many individuals. In 1765 General Warburton's agent, Mr Hughes, decided to lease the quarry workings to about eighty of them, at an annual rent of one pound. Warburton introduced the traditional names given to the various sizes of slates (Empresses, Queens, Duchesses, Countesses, Ladies), but his income from the ownership of the quarry was clearly minimal.

(Left) The west front of the medieval house at Penrhyn

(Below, left) The west front after it was modernised by Samuel Wyatt after 1782; drawings by Moses Griffith

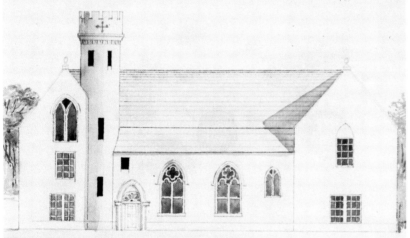

(Opposite page) Richard Pennant (1739– 1808), by Henry Thomson (No.58, Dining Room). He transformed the Penrhyn estate by his agricultural improvements and developed the slate quarries. The map he points to shows the new, more direct route of the road he built via Capel Curig to Holyhead

Very soon after he succeeded, Richard Pennant called in these leases and took the management of the quarry in hand. He removed quantities of overburden and slate waste, and built a new road from the quarry to the mouth of the River Cegin, later to be extended south down the Nant Ffrancon, and through the Ogwen valley to Capel Curig. On his arrival he found that the quarry could muster only four carts for the carriage of the slate, and by engaging farm tenants and labourers in the work he increased this to 100. At the river mouth he established Port (or Porth) Penrhyn from 1786. Here, the slates were embarked for shipment to other parts of Britain and Ireland.

Richard Pennant's reforms and later mechanisation greatly increased the output of the quarry, but the work of the quarrymen remained fundamentally unchanged. A slate block had first to be detached from the quarry face, by wedges and later explosive charges, inserted by men often dangling on ropes over precipitous drops. The detached blocks were then cleaved and divided ('pillared') into smaller blocks, and finally split and dressed by hand in sheds some distance away.

The Wyatts played a leading role in the marketing of the slate. In 1801 Lord Penrhyn (as he had by then become) signed an agreement with Samuel

A slate pyramid in Llandygai churchyard commemorates several generations of the Wyatt family of Lime Grove, who served the Penrhyn estate from the late eighteenth century

A view of Penrhyn c.1785, showing the new house (left) and park gateway (right) by Samuel Wyatt

Worthington, Michael Humble and Samuel Holland, all of Liverpool, by which these individuals were to be supplied with all the slates from Penrhyn quarry at specified rates '. . . excepting all such slates as Samuel Wyatt or James Wyatt of London, architects, shall or may want within business respectively'.[5] Samuel used it for the fittings of the new stables at Holkham, Norfolk, and seems to have taken a positive interest in extending the range of its use, for shelves, cisterns, lavatory seats and window-sills. At Shugborough he clad the entire house in squared Penrhyn slates painted to resemble ashlar (or squared stone), and constructed a portico of columns constructed of thin fillets of slate around a wooden core.

The smoothness of properly split and ground slate makes it an ideal writing surface, from which marks in chalk can be easily erased. The gradual spread of education to all classes from the later eighteenth century, in which Pennant himself played a part as a builder of schools, created an enormous demand for 'blackboards' large and small that he sought to satisfy. On the wharf at Port Penrhyn, a manufactory was established for the finishing and framing of writing-slates. 'Previously, we were entirely supplied from *Switzerland*', wrote Thomas Pennant, but 'that trade has now ceased;

the *Swiss* manufacturers are become bankrupt.'[6] Every year 136,000 writing slates were produced at Port Penrhyn, consuming 3,000 feet of timber for the frames, and employing up to thirty men.

In 1783, on the recommendation of Charles James Fox, Pennant was created Baron Penrhyn of Penrhyn, County Louth, an Irish title which did not prevent him from sitting as a member of the Commons. (To avoid confusion with Edward Gordon, 1st Lord Penrhyn of Llandegai, he is here referred to as Richard Pennant throughout.) From 1784 to 1790 he again represented Liverpool and in that time made thirty speeches, all on the Liverpool trade and the West Indies, leading the planters' defence of the slave trade with such vigour that he was known as the 'Chairman of the West Indian Merchants'.

Richard Pennant's management of the family's Jamaican property is well documented and although he never visited the island – a world apart from the mountains of Caernarfonshire – he was remarkably well informed, and kept in close touch with his representatives on the island.

Pennant was particularly adept at devising new variations to the reciprocal Triangular Trade, upon which the success of the West Indian sugar industry depended. In 1782, he was writing to Jamaica offer-

A watercolour view of Richard Pennant's Jamaican estates, one of six possibly by Richard Clevely (Passage to the Keep Bedrooms)

ing 'Mechanicks … Carpenters, Smiths, Coopers, Bricklayers, etc, etc' and, remarkably, the slaves developed a partiality to herrings shipped from Britain. Manure was also sent on the returning ships, and Pennant, the true entrepreneur, was alive to the prospects for diversification. He had the foresight to predict the importance of cotton many years before it replaced sugar as the most important crop traded across the Atlantic, and that there was money to be made from supplying the booming Lancashire cotton factories nearby. 'The cotton manufacturers are increasing greatly', he wrote to his attorney in 1782, 'which will make a large demand for cotton and create good prices – are any of my lands proper for cotton?'[7] He also suggested indigo, and tried, unsuccessfully, to create a market in Jamaica and southern North America for his slates.

This talent for complementary enterprises led to a number of mutually supporting activities on the Caernarfonshire estate. The leading figure in most of these was Samuel Worthington, the merchant with whom Pennant signed an agreement in 1796 allowing him to search for minerals on the estate. Worthington found manganese and zinc ores (for bleaching and pigments respectively), ochre (also for pigments) and extracted chert and quartz from

the base of Carnedd Llywelyn near the slate quarry. With flints shipped on the slate vessels returning from Ireland, these materials were processed for the ceramic industry at a mill on the River Ogwen, and kilns by the port. Their principal destination was the Herculaneum pottery in Liverpool, in which Messrs Humble and Holland, the distributors of the Penrhyn slate, were founding partners. Once the pottery had built its own kilns, in 1818, those at Port Penrhyn were employed for burning lime, probably used in the construction of Hopper's castle (see Chapter Three).

The principal product continued to be slate, and the combined energies of Richard Pennant and Benjamin Wyatt were irresistible, despite the most adverse conditions. When war broke out against France in 1793, and the prime minister, William Pitt, imposed a crippling tax on all slate carried coastwise, the workforce at the quarry slumped from six hundred to a little over one hundred. 'The spirit of building', which had fuelled the demand for slate over the past decade, was broken, said the Penrhyn 'slate reeve' (or foreman), William Williams. The redundant quarrymen were pressed into service in a new venture, the creation of an iron tramway from the quarry to the port, 6 miles long and falling through 500 feet, the fall accommodated

A farmer's house built by Benjamin Wyatt on the Penrhyn estate

by means of four inclined planes along the way. Work was put in hand to deepen the port itself to enable it to take larger vessels, once the trade recovered. The tramway, which was to operate until replaced by a steam railway in 1874, vastly increased the efficiency and capacity of the operation in the early decades of the nineteenth century; 12 men and 16 horses could now transport a greater annual quantity to the port than 140 men with 400 horses had done before the tramway was built. At the same time, William Williams set about the excavation of proper working 'galleries' in the quarry faces.

Whilst the building trade at large was supplied with ever-increasing quantities of Penrhyn slate, Pennant and the Wyatts were themselves building on a considerable scale. While Samuel Wyatt was supervising the construction of the new castle, he also designed a classical villa near the port known as 'Lime Grove' for the agent to the estate; his brother Benjamin, who held that post from 1786, acted as architect for a whole series of buildings which, while perhaps less sophisticated, were none the less both useful and delightful. Soon after his appointment Benjamin Wyatt designed a Neo-classical cattle shed in the park, complete with a Doric colonnade, and a dairy farm near the quarry at Penisa'rnant, which combined the Neo-classical and Gothic styles. Equipped with cool slate slabs and furnished with Wedgwood pottery, the dairy was surrounded by a pleasure ground whose ornaments included 'a small stool made to imitate a giant mushroom. An apiary well contrived with straw hive and glass one [sic]: at the back of the house . . . a curious piggery and poultry yard, with a fountain playing in one of the courts'.[8] A tunnel was built under the new road so that the pigs could reach the mountain pasture.

Where the newly created parkland touched the sea, between the mouths of the rivers Ogwen and Cegin, Benjamin Wyatt built a splendid marine bath for bathing in heated sea water, at the end of an 'artifical mole'. 'There is a dressing room each side, or rather an undressing room, one for the ladies and the other for the gentlemen'. The route to the baths from the castle, 'by an amazing high carriage terrace', became an important feature of the park,

Ogwen Bank, the Gothic villa built by Richard Pennant near his slate quarries to designs by Benjamin Wyatt, c.1790; coloured aquatint by J. Havell

much enjoyed by visitors, who could rest on the way at 'an elegant little cottage of her ladyship . . . overun [sic] with Passion flowers and beautiful creepers of various kinds'[9] and which included a room decorated with caricature prints.

To the tourist influenced by contemporary Romanticism, who was marooned at home by the wars in Europe, the great industrial ventures of the late-eighteenth century – from Coalbrookdale in Shropshire to Matthew Boulton's celebrated Soho works in Birmingham – became almost as important destinations as the Sublime scenery of mountains and valleys. Penrhyn had both industry and landscape, and Pennant and Wyatt were quick to cater for this new interest. They built a new hotel at Capel Curig for visitors to Snowdon, and another by Port Penrhyn, the Penrhyn Arms, for the accommodation of visitors to the castle and the quarry. Both were also on the emergent main route to Ireland via Holyhead. Favoured visitors to the quarry could rest at Lady Penrhyn's Gothic villa at Ogwen Bank (also by Benjamin Wyatt).

The printed descriptions of the quarry are legion. Early on they are matter-of-fact, but from around 1800 the usual response was thus: 'Here I found several immense openings, with sides and bottoms, as rude as imagination can paint, that had been formed in getting the slate. On first surveying them, a degree of surprise is excited, how such yawning chasms could have been formed by any but the immediate operations of Nature.'[10]

Sadly, little of Richard Pennant's built legacy remains. In 1797 another Wyatt, Lewis William, son of Benjamin, exhibited a series of drawings at the Royal Academy of buildings on the Penrhyn estate designed by his father and his uncle Samuel. He went on to publish, in 1800–1, *A Collection of Architectural Designs ... Executed in a Variety of Buildings, upon the Estate of the Right. Hon. Lord Penrhyn*. None of the buildings illustrated survives.

Pennant died at Winnington in 1808, but his body was brought home to Llandygai along the road he had created. Only Pennant's monument, by Richard Westmacott, set up at his widow's instigation in Llandegai church in 1821, does justice to his achievements. It consists of a sarcophagus, flanked by heroic figures of a quarryman and a peasant girl with her distaff, and with a frieze of four groups of putti, emblematic of the state of the country before his succession, and his improvements in slate quarrying, education and agriculture.

'About 40 years ago', wrote Richard Llwyd in

The monument to Richard Pennant in Llandygai church by Richard Westmacott features the figures of a quarryman and a peasant girl with her distaff in recognition of his industrial and agricultural achievements

1832, 'this part of the country bore a most wild, barren, and uncultivated appearance, but it is now covered with handsome villas, well built farm houses, neat cottages, rich meadows, well-cultivated fields, and flourishing plantations; bridges have been built, new roads made, bogs and swampy grounds drained and cultivated, neat fences raised, and barren rocks covered with woods. In fact, what has been accomplished in this neighbourhood in so short a space of time may be denominated a new creation, and that principally by means of one active and noble-minded individual who disposed of his vast resources in various acts of improvement; and by doing so gave employment to hundreds of his fellow-creatures, who were thus rendered comfortable and happy.'[11]

Lady Penrhyn survived her husband by eight years, and continued to live at Penrhyn. Their marriage was childless, but she is said to have been less than delighted when her husband left the property on his death in 1808 to his cousin, George Hay Dawkins, although for her lifetime she enjoyed the income from the quarry. Lord Penrhyn's will provided annuities to her lady's maid for the welfare of her ladyship's three pug dogs and to the groom for the care of seven horses and seven dogs, but animal lover though she evidently was, these legacies can hardly have provided much consolation in her years of widowhood.

NOTES

1 A. H. Dodd, *A History of Caernarvonshire*, 1968, p.232.

2 Thomas Pennant, op. cit., iii, p.86.

3 Peter Ellis-Jones, 'The Wyatts of Lime Grove, Llandegai', *Trans. Caernarvonshire Historical Society*, xlii, 1981.

4 Nicholas Owen, *Caernarvonshire, a sketch of its history*, 1792, p.30.

5 Penrhyn MSS, UCNW, 2034.

6 op. cit., iii, p.87.

7 Penrhyn MSS, UCNW, 1248–58.

8 Richard Fenton, *Tour in Carnarvon*, July 1813. Cardiff City Library MSS, published in *Archaeologia Cambrensis*, xvii, 1917.

9 Ibid.

10 W. Bingley, *Excursions in North Wales*, 1798, i, p.179.

11 '*The History of Wales*', revised and corrected with '*Topographical Notices*', 1832, p.35.

CHAPTER THREE
THE BUILDING OF THE CASTLE

George Hay Dawkins (1764–1840) took up his inheritance on the death of Lady Penrhyn in 1816, assuming the additional name and arms of Pennant in accordance with his benefactor's will. He was the second son of Henry Dawkins II of Standlynch, Wiltshire, and of Over Norton, Oxfordshire, and his wife Lady Juliana Colyear, daughter of the 2nd Earl of Portmore. Dawkins was also the great-great-grandson of Gifford Pennant of Jamaica. His first wife, the Hon. Sophia Mary Maude, bore him two daughters but probably never set eyes on Penrhyn. She died at the age of 40, after only five years of marriage, in 1812. Two years later Dawkins married Elizabeth, daughter of the Hon. William Henry Bouverie, brother of the 2nd Earl of Radnor.

It is tantalising that we know so little of the life of a man who could call into being so fantastic and original a building as Penrhyn Castle. Like his benefactor before him he was a Member of Parliament, for Newark in Nottinghamshire in 1814–18 and New Romney in Kent in 1820–30. From the little evidence that does survive he comes across as a reserved, almost austere, character, driven by what the German traveller and horticulturalist Prince Herman von Pückler-Muskau, visiting Penrhyn during its construction, described as 'building-mania … this wealthy man lives with his family in a humble cottage in the neighbourhood, with a small establishment; he feasts once a week on the sight of his fairy castle, which, after the long continuation of such simple habits, he will probably never bring himself to inhabit. It appeared to give him great pleasure to show and explain everything to me, and I experienced no less from his enthusiasm, which was agreeable and becoming in a man otherwise cold.'[1]

In Parliament Dawkins-Pennant consistently opposed the movement for reform of the electoral system that led to the Great Reform Bill of 1832, and the emancipation of slaves within the British Empire. (He received compensation of £14,683 for the 764 slaves on his estates, when this measure was effected in 1833.)

Dawkins-Pennant moved to Penrhyn the year after Waterloo had put an end to two decades of war. He had had eight years in which to contemplate improvements. As the result of the war and its taxes, unemployment and destitution were serious problems in Caernarfonshire, as elsewhere. In 1818 for the first time a nightly patrol had to be established in Bangor for the control of vagrants, and the Select Committee on Telford's Holyhead Road urged that the work be accelerated, both to take advantage of cheap labour and for the sake of employing the large numbers out of work. It is not hard to imagine Dawkins-Pennant seeing an opportunity as well as a duty in this situation.

However, to see the building of Penrhyn Castle merely as an exercise in job-creation would be absurd, for there were a number of other influences that must have borne on Dawkins-Pennant at this time. The house he had inherited in 1808 was still barely thirty years old, and not insubstantial, but if in 1798 it could have been faintly praised as 'a good specimen of the military Gothic',[2] it was now fast becoming unfashionable. One writer was to compare it unfavourably with Lime Grove, the agent's house, which 'in point of chasteness and technical purity' was deemed superior. Meanwhile, along the coast at Abergele, Lloyd Bamford Hesketh had been building himself a castle called Gwrych, in many ways the most successful Picturesque building of all. 'The site is lofty', wrote C. F. Cliffe in 1851, 'and the structure, which is a mimic one to a considerable extent, has been built for effect. It is said to be 480 yds. long, with a splendid terrace in front. There are 18 towers, the largest of which is 93 ft. high.'[3] Gwrych was completed c.1816, but it was only the nearest of a great number of new castles to have been thrown up in the first years of the nineteenth century (see Appendix).

Pückler-Muskau was one of those who witnessed the building of the new Penrhyn Castle, and in his astonishment at the scale of the enterprise he mused on the castles of William the Conqueror's time: 'What could then be accomplished only by a mighty monarch is now executed, as a plaything, – only with increased size, magnificence and expense, – by a simple country-gentleman, whose father very likely sold cheeses'.[4]

In one major respect he was wrong. Dawkins-Pennant's father had owned a substantial country house that had been bought by the nation for the descendants of Lord Nelson; his aunt, Lady Caroline Colyear, had married the 1st Lord Scarsdale, builder of Kedleston Hall in Derbyshire, and his uncle, James Dawkins, had led the expedition that rediscovered the ruined cities of Baalbec and Palmyra in 1751. The selling of cheeses did not figure in this pedigree. On the contrary, the fusion of these elements – antiquarianism, architectural patronage on the grand scale, two West Indian fortunes and a burgeoning agricultural estate and industrial enterprise – was tantamount to alchemy.

It is not clear how Dawkins-Pennant came to appoint Thomas Hopper (1776–1856) as his architect; prior to Penrhyn (and Gosford, Co. Armagh, begun slightly earlier) his country-house work had been confined to remodellings and alterations. His most significant commission by far had been the construction of a new conservatory for the Prince of Wales at Carlton House in London in 1807, a fantasia on the chapel of Henry VII in Westminster Abbey, replete with ancient Welsh heraldry and vaulted in cast iron.

In October 1817 an unremarkable payment is recorded in Dawkins-Pennant's Cash Book: 'John Williams Coachman, for a Xmas box' – five shillings. Curiously, the following May there occurs the further entry: 'To John Williams, Coachman of the Prince Regent, a Xmas box', again five shillings. Williams was similarly rewarded (and described) in July 1820, by which time work was proceeding on the new castle. If Williams actually brought the Prince to Penrhyn at these times, the recom-

mendation of Thomas Hopper must have come with him.

It seems unlikely that Hopper was responsible for the two anonymous proposal drawings that survive, one for a great hall and the other a perspective from the south west. Although the perspective prefigures the shape of the principal block, and the hall design shows some of the devices later employed by Hopper, the drawings have none of the boldness and assurance of his executed work, and must represent a rejected proposal by a lesser architect.

What must be by Hopper is a single, unsigned plan inscribed 'Ground Plan of Penrhyn Castle/ Dawkins Pennant Esqre', but not dated. Most of this plan was adopted; the major differences lie at the northern end of the west front, where a massive square block with circular towers at the corners was proposed, containing on one side a 'Great Drawing Room' 76 by 36 feet and lit by five windows facing south. Even at Penrhyn this would have been a prodigious room, and it is not known whether it was ever begun, but its omission may explain the somewhat inarticulate appearance of this elevation today. Hopper certainly lived up to his famous dictum that 'it is an architect's business to understand all styles and to be prejudiced in favour of none', but the reasons for the choice of the 'Norman' style at Penrhyn are not obvious. Whereas at Gosford, Co. Armagh, where Hopper also began a new castle in 1820, the Norman style must have seemed the obvious choice in an Ireland conquered by Strongbow, in north Wales the conquerors' style was the late thirteenth-century Gothic of the great royal castles built by the Plantagenet Edward I at

(Right) The north front; one of a series of lithographs of the interior and exterior of Penrhyn commissioned from G. Hawkins by Col. Douglas-Pennant

(Right, below) An early proposal drawing of the south-west elevation, which was not executed

(Left, top) George Hay Dawkins-Pennant (1764– 1840), the builder of the castle. Posthumous miniature by C. J. Basébe after John Jackson, 1841 (private collection)

(Left, bottom) Thomas Hopper (1776–1856), the architect of the castle; lithograph after a bust by J. Ternouth, 1838

Caernarfon and Conwy. Here, perhaps, an 'earlier' style was deliberately used 'to suggest a more ancient, and therefore native, lineage'.[5]

How much of the design was left to Hopper, and how much was stipulated by his client? The view of one early visitor that 'Mr Pennant has delivered himself over entirely to his Architect, who delights in rearing a Mass of Building to his own [taste], without the slightest consideration for the comfort of the family',[6] cannot be credited, even when Dawkins-Pennant's son-in-law said jokingly, 'Mr Hopper used to come in after breakfast and ask leave to add another tower',[7] and Capt. Francis Maude, his brother-in-law from his first marriage, recalled how Dawkins-Pennant once said to him, 'they want to add a *Keep* out there Francis, I don't know what they mean by it'.[8] The evidence of the surviving letters from Hopper to his client – albeit concerned with the fitting-out rather than the construction – points rather to a very close collaboration in the minutiae of the project.

The building chronology has been confused by writers on Penrhyn, but Pückler-Muskau's statement in 1828 that 'it is now seven years since the Castle was begun . . . and it will probably take four years more to complete it',[9] seems to be more or less accurate on both counts. The earliest date seems to be April 1819, when William Baxter, 'who superintends the works carrying on at Penrhyn Castle',[10] was sent to Penmon on Anglesey to agree prices for stone from a number of quarries around the promontory. When the thirteen-year-old Princess Victoria visited in 1832, she found the castle 'not near finished yet',[11] and although the number of visitors rose dramatically from 1833, the furnishings were not yet complete in the early months of 1835,

when Hopper was still preoccupied with candelabra and other fittings.

The work began with the construction of a new park wall, 7 miles in circuit, which displaced six farms and the main road, which Dawkins-Pennant re-routed. The wall was built of rubble stones from the Cochwillan and other quarries, and topped with a coping of rough Penrhyn blue slate slabs laid on edge. The Grand Lodge was begun, possibly by the masons recently employed on Lord Anglesey's column at Llanfairpwll, and the massive gates hung. Yards for the carpenters and masons were established (where the car-park is today) and by July 1819 the carpenters were at work, presumably preparing the scaffolding. The walls of the new castle were probably rising by 1821.

For the next few years the accounts fall silent, but by October 1826 the Library Tower, the Oak Tower and the Grand Hall were all completed and were being slated with 'Queens' from the quarry. A drawing of this date by Dawkins-Pennant's eighteen-year-old daughter, Juliana, shows no sign of the Keep. While the works were in progress, she went on a sketching tour which took in Warwick Castle (where she drew Guy's Tower), and Charlecote church. Two years later, Pückler-Muskau was shown the 'eating hall' [the Grand Hall], by the architect himself, and was able to describe many of

the out-offices, in particular the laundry. The plasterers were on site by the spring of 1830, when 400 bushels of cow hair were delivered, and lime was brought from the kilns at Port Penrhyn. In June and July 292 polished plates of glass arrived from the Ravenshead works of J. Crockford & Co., and from a drawing dated 9 October, it appears that the Keep and the other principal towers had risen to their full height. The drawing shows the outline of the stables in a dotted line, and these clearly constituted the last major phase of work, between August 1831 and June 1833. The very large quantity of slate slabs delivered from the quarry in 1834 presumably included those used for the stalls and mangers, as well as for paving the yards.

Throughout the building period there are large numbers of accounts for building stone, from the Anglesey limestone quarries around Penmon, Red Wharf Bay and Moelfre, to an almost equally large number of suppliers. The external walling is not, as has often been suggested, of 'Mona Marble' (a serpentinite used for some of the chimney-pieces), but of Penmon limestone, a dark grey or black stone with many large fossils and other defects. In view of these drawbacks the exceptionally fine jointing – in places even narrower than can be found in the best freestone ashlar work – speaks highly of the master masons, of whom Nathan Ryan, Griff Jones and

(Right) The west front

(Opposite page) An aerial view of the castle, showing the principal elements: the Keep (left) containing family apartments, the State Apartments (centre), and the Staff Quarters and Stables (right)

A window in the Keep, showing the Norman zig-zag motif and the very finely jointed Penmon limestone walls

William Pritchard are named in the accounts. From the frequency and size of his payments on account, one Edward Jones of Llandygai appears to have been the principal contractor.

Chimney-pieces were supplied by Thomas Crisp in 1833–4. The name of the master plasterer has not emerged, but the work is of such high quality that the firm of the leading plaster craftsman of the day, Francis Bernasconi, has been suggested. Robert Offer, a native of Bath who died at Bangor in 1829 and was described as 'many years foreman of the plasterers at Penrhyn Castle', may not have been responsible for the ornamental work.

Penrhyn Castle can be seen as the masterpiece of the stonemasons and carpenters of North Wales in any period. 'Mr Pennant deserves the thanks and admiration of every friend of Wales', wrote Angharad Llwyd in 1832, 'for the almost exclusive encouragement he has given to the native artificers of every kind ...',[12] and Adela Douglas-Pennant later wrote that 'the entire work was carried out by local workmen under the superintendence of the architect Mr Hopper'.[13] She adds that most of the Norman furniture was made by the estate carpenters. The fact that none of the oak columns, the

dadoes and the neo-Norman furniture is carved from the solid, but rather composed of applied, pre-carved, repeated elements gives credence to this claim. Taken together, this combination on the grandest scale of Welsh oak, limestone, slate and marble shaped by 'native skill' can be seen as the expression of pride in the raw materials of his adopted region by a rich squire who was also a prodigious 'extractor'.

Hopper employed not only local craftsmen, but in Thomas Willement the leading stained-glass designer in Britain. Willement supplied superb glass, featuring the signs of the zodiac, for the Grand

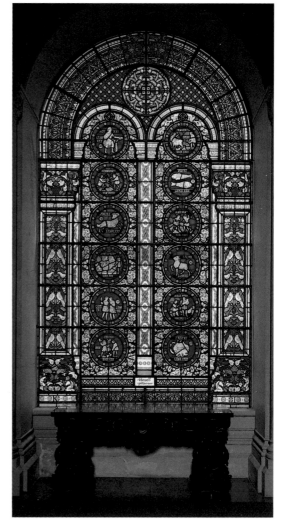

Hall, and may have provided designs for the decoration of the Dining Room. As Heraldic Artist to George IV, he must surely have had a say in the heraldic programme as a whole, but, surprisingly, he was not asked to supply armorial glass; that was provided by David Evans of Shrewsbury.

The total cost of the work is not definitively recorded, and early estimates varied considerably. It can, however, hardly have been less than the £123,000 suggested by Catherine Sinclair, who describes Penrhyn in her book *Hill and Valley* (1839). Money was certainly not a problem for Dawkins-Pennant. At his death in 1840, his income was estimated at £80,000 per annum, and his personal property 'sworn under £600,000'.

Penrhyn is to such an extent unique that it has persistently defied description or categorisation. 'To wander through the wondrous halls of Penrhyn', wrote Louisa Stuart Costello in 1845, 'is like struggling along in a bewildered dream occasioned by having studied some elaborate work on the early buildings of the Saxons or Normans.'[14] To early visitors, whether they thought it 'Saxon', 'Norman', 'Roman', or 'one of the most complete castellated baronial mansions in the kingdom', Penrhyn was never unimpressive, and always counted a success. Though Hopper's building would not

for an instant deceive anyone with an idea of what a Norman castle actually looked like, in his compilation of architectural types and decorative elements spanning at least three medieval centuries, he produced a castle that was at once more 'archaeological' than its near-contemporaries, and yet eminently Picturesque. Of course, the site was exceptional, and ancient, but the distant view of the clear and commanding outline of the Keep suggests a strategic importance it never had. In the distant landscape it makes for a composition worthy of the seventeenth-century French landscapist Claude, and it is no surprise that more than sixty engraved views of the castle and its surroundings were published in the thirty years following its completion, and countless drawings and watercolours.

Closer to hand, given the extreme length of the building and the way that the ground slopes away on all sides, almost no complete 'elevation' can be seen. The fact that the most frequent views of the exterior are oblique also offered Hopper the greatest scope for deploying his towers for compositional effect. The relationship between the Keep and the other, lesser towers and turrets frequently disguises the distances between them.

In all its massiveness and cyclopean scale, Penrhyn partakes of the Romantic notion of the

(Right) The east front; lithograph by G. Hawkins

(Left) Willement's stained glass in the Grand Hall

25

The Keep

Sublime, the infinite or immeasurable, perhaps best appreciated at the foot of the Keep. Most importantly, despite the necessity for adequate windows in place of loopholes and arrow slits, the castle also looks defensible. No other late Georgian castle-builders went to such trouble in this respect; most would have been content, for example, with conventional – perhaps mildly Gothicised – stables, where Hopper and Dawkins-Pennant threw up a high curtain wall with four titanic towers complete with 'murder holes'. Penrhyn was a genuinely secure fortress; secure also, therefore, from Pugin's famous swipe at modern castles: 'who would hammer against nailed portals', he asked in 1841, 'when he could kick his way through the greenhouse?'[15] Whether the fortification of Penrhyn was due simply to a desire for historical accuracy or to actual fears of a possible siege is a matter for speculation.

The choice of an exotic style – whether Norman, Gothic or (as at Brighton Pavilion) 'Hindoo' – presented architects with formidable technical challenges, not the least of which was the placing of chimneys. At Penrhyn, with 70 roofs of sharply

differing heights, Hopper was forced to distribute the smoke from his fireplaces by the most tortuous and unlikely routes (no fewer than seventeen flues converge in the upper storeys of the Housemaids' Tower, for instance), but in some respects he was able to draw on new technology. The ducted hot-air system which heated the Grand Hall and neighbouring rooms was among the first to be installed in mainland Britain.

One of the fantastically decorated composition-stone luminaires in the Grand Hall

Piped water was a rarer luxury. Miss Sinclair writes that 'in each dressing-room, instead of a window-seat, a bath is placed, with pipes of hot and cold water perpetually ready ... It is to be hoped that the progress of luxury and comfort will at last introduce this indulgence into every house and dressing-room in England.'[16] Water-closets were lavishly provided, some of them on the upper floors spectacularly top-lit by lofty skylights or lanterns.

Lighting was at first by oil; gas fittings were subsequently installed, which were replaced with electricity in 1927–8 by A.V.Gifkins & Co. of Victoria St, Westminster. Most of the bronze lamps are of the type named after the Swiss inventor Aimé Argand, and they were not uncommon in British houses by the 1820s. By his patent, the oil (which from 1834 was generally colza oil from crushed rape-seeds, later superseded by paraffin or naptha) was fed by gravity from a font or reservoir, and the etched glass funnels accelerated the flow of air to the cylindrical wick in the tubular metal burner. The provision of more than one burner minimised the shadow cast by the reservoir.

The pursuit of sources for the design of the castle, its interiors and furnishings, may never end. There seems little doubt, however, that the Keep is derived from that of Hedingham Castle in Essex, where Hopper served as County Surveyor for forty years. In the arrangements of the towers, and particularly the northern (entrance) elevation of the stable block, there are close similarities with Raglan Castle in Gwent. Among more recent castles, Eastnor in Herefordshire (by Robert Smirke, c.1812–20), despite its basic symmetry, prefigures Penrhyn in the play of square and round towers, and especially in the use of tall, round towers leading the eye round each angle.

For the interior, medieval precedents are less easy to find for the architecture than for the decoration, even in the case of the Grand Hall (sometimes compared with the nave of Durham Cathedral). For precedents in the revived Norman style, one authority has proposed a volume of stage designs for the Berlin Theatre by Karl Schinkel, published in 1819–24.[17]

Perhaps closer still, since they actually show domestic interiors in the Norman style, are the unexecuted designs for Lea Castle, Worcestershire, by John Carter, produced a year before his death in 1818. An unsuccessful architect, Carter made his name as a draughtsman and engraver of medieval buildings and their decoration. His masterpiece was *The Ancient Architecture of England* (1795–1814), a compendium of engraved plates of details mainly from ecclesiastical buildings, which has as much of the character of a pattern-book as a purely anti-quarian treatise. It was almost certainly a major source of designs for the decoration of columns, capitals, arches and doorways at Penrhyn (Daw-kins-Pennant's own copy survives in the Library).

One book that was unquestionably drawn upon was Joseph Strutt's *Sports and Pastimes of the English People* (1801), a scholarly survey of the popular

A plate showing details from Shireburn Minster, Dorset, taken from John Carter's 'Ancient Architecture of England', which inspired much of the decoration at Penrhyn

recreations of 'Olden Time' with illustrations chiefly taken from the margins of medieval manuscripts. Many of these were copied directly for the carved decoration at Penrhyn. Strutt's work also provided valuable source material for Sir Walter Scott's *Ivanhoe*, published in 1820, the year Penrhyn was begun. Scott and Hopper faced similar difficulties in reconstructing the Middle Ages, and just as the dialogue in *Ivanhoe* was not written 'in Anglo-Saxon or in Norman French', Hopper allowed his castle the anachronisms of fitted carpets, water closets and plate glass.

Dawkins-Pennant indulged to the full Hopper's considerable ingenuity in designing new furniture and carpets in a 'Norman' style. For, surprisingly,

Joseph Strutt's 'Sports and Pastimes' provided the inspiration for the carving on the Library chimney-piece

he seems not to have shared the passion for collecting 'baronial' furniture and fittings that affected many other castle-builders of the time.

Some time after the principal rooms at Penrhyn were finished, Col. Douglas-Pennant commissioned a series of lithographs illustrating some of them, along with several views of the exterior, from the little-known printmaker G. Hawkins. It seems odd that his invaluable series of views was not intended for publication with commentaries, as was done for Fonthill in Wiltshire in 1823 and for Toddington in Gloucestershire in 1840. Dawkins-Pennant died in December 1840, only a few years after his castle was completed, and was buried in the Dawkins family vault at Chipping Norton in Oxfordshire. Perhaps if he had had a little longer to enjoy his creation before his death, he would have published such a volume, and prevented so much later speculation.

NOTES

1 *Tour in England*, i, p.133.

2 W. Bingley, op. cit., p.132.

3 *The Book of North Wales*, 1851, p.95.

4 *Travels of a German Prince*, i, 1828.

5 Timothy Mowl, 'The Norman Revival in British Architecture 1790–1870', PhD thesis, Oxford Univ., 1981, p.209.

6 Lord Hatherton of Teddesley, *Journal*, Sept. 1832; Staffs. Record Office MS D/260/M/F/5/26/8.

7 Adela Douglas-Pennant, *Memoir*.

8 Ibid.

9 *Tour in England*, i, 1832: entry for 2 August 1828.

10 Penrhyn MSS, UCNW: Baxter received his first payment as Clerk of Works the following month, and held the post until his death in 1840.

11 Journal for September 1832. Royal Archives.

12 *A History of the Island of Mona*, Prize Essay, Beaumaris Eisteddfod, 1832, p.12.

13 Adela Douglas-Pennant, *Memoir*.

14 *The Falls, Lakes and Mountains of North Wales*, 1845, p.86.

15 A. W. N. Pugin, *The True Principles of Pointed or Christian Architecture*, 1841, p.59.

16 *Hill and Valley*, 1833, p.132.

17 Hague, Douglas B., 'Penrhyn Castle', *Trans. Caernarvonshire Historical Society*, xx, 1959, p.41.

CHAPTER FOUR
THE DOUGLAS-PENNANTS OF PENRHYN

George Dawkins-Pennant had no children by his second marriage, and so his two daughters (known as the 'Slate Queens', or the Queen of Diamonds and the Queen of Hearts) were his heirs. The elder, Juliana Isabella Mary, who inherited Penrhyn, was married in 1833 to Edward Gordon Douglas (1800–86), captain in the Grenadier Guards, and grandson of the 14th Earl of Morton; he was promoted colonel the following year. In 1824 Edward Douglas had been one of a crew of six officers who for a bet had rowed a wherry from Oxford to Westminster in under sixteen hours. According to his youngest daughter, Adela, this younger-son-of-a-younger-son hesitated to propose to so great an heiress, but was encouraged by Mrs Dawkins-Pennant, who was his first cousin. Her husband seems to have found the idea not to his liking and after a stormy interview, Capt. Douglas removed himself and his luggage to the Penrhyn Arms Hotel. The marriage eventually took place at St. Marylebone, and 150 workmen sat down to supper in their honour at Port Penrhyn, consuming 473 quarts of ale in the process. The couple lived in Yorkshire until Dawkins-Pennant's death in 1840.

In 1841, in accordance with Dawkins-Pennant's will, they became the Hon. Edward and Mrs Douglas-Pennant, and in that year Col. Douglas-Pennant was elected as MP for Carnarvonshire (which he continued to represent until elevated to the peerage in 1866). The following winter, Juliana caught a chill while climbing Snowdon, having lent her cloak to another of the party. The ailment worsened and on the advice of the surgeon Sir Prescott Hewett, the family set out for the Riviera to effect a cure. Juliana caught a fresh chill at Pisa and died there in April 1842.

In 1846 Col. Douglas-Pennant took as his second wife Lady Maria Louisa Fitzroy, daughter of the 5th Duke of Grafton, having met her hunting at his Northamptonshire seat, Wicken Park (which he had leased from the Mordaunt family in 1840 and later bought). Douglas-Pennant and his family lived at Penrhyn for only part of the year, residing principally in August and from October to Christmas. The rest of the year was spent at Wicken and at Mortimer House in Halkin Street, Belgravia, the family's London home from 1859. The family's whereabouts dictated the hours during which the castle was opened to the public (tickets were sold at the Penrhyn Arms and other local hotels). Julius Rodenberg described his arrival in 1856:

The whole castle ground was full of people – ladies with leather gloves, not unlike fencing gloves, and blue silk parasols above their straw hats; gentlemen in checked caps, their necks encased in stiff collars – for a gentleman cannot make himself completely comfortable, even when on holiday. The curiosity of this monstrous crowd was satisfied in batches: every quarter of an hour the gate opened, to let two dozen out and another two dozen in. In the meantime I had leisure to study the coat of arms on the door. It was an antelope driven by a scourge with the inscription: *Aequo Animo*... Truly it required great equanimity to allow oneself to be herded through a castle with 24 gentlemen by a withered, gloomy, suspicious old woman, and a castle of exquisite splendour, giving evidence of the warmest enjoyment of the best things in life.[1]

Col. Douglas-Pennant added greatly to the Penrhyn estate (see Chapter Eight), especially in the Meillionydd district of the Llŷn Peninsula, and to the collection of pictures (see Chapter Five). In 1859 he entertained the Queen and Prince Albert at the castle. They planted trees in the grounds, toured the Nant Ffrancon valley and the slate quarry, and after dinner at the castle heard the Llanllechid choir sing choruses from the *Messiah* in Welsh in the Grand Hall. Douglas-Pennant's daughter, Adela, later recalled the visit:

A man was specially had down from Miller's the great lamp shop in London, to see after the lighting of the house during the Royal visit, instead of trusting to the services of the ordinary "lamp man" of the House. This man deserted his duties, to see the arrival of the Royal guests and omitted to light the corkscrew staircase up to the keep, so that when my mother took the Queen to her room, she found the stairs in complete darkness. My Mother begged the Queen to wait while she ran upstairs for a light, but on returning to the head of the steps, she found the Queen had laughingly groped her way up behind her in the dark.[2]

Col. Douglas-Pennant was created 1st Baron Penrhyn of Llandegai in 1866. Never a frequent speaker in either House, none the less he was constantly busy in committees. He was well acquainted with Gladstone, and their political differences did not prevent Mrs Gladstone's frequent presence at Penrhyn, for the families had much in common. Gladstone's father had been a Liverpool merchant who owned substantial sugar plantations in the West Indies. Like Lord Penrhyn's father-in-law, Gladstone had begun his political career as MP for Newark and in his maiden speech in 1833 he had stoutly defended the West Indian interest. The Gladstones habitually spent a month's holiday along the coast at Penmaenmawr, and while staying there in September 1861,

Juliana Isabella Dawkins-Pennant (1808–42). The heir to the Penrhyn estate, she married Edward Douglas in 1833. Miniature by Adam Buck

(Right) A group of family and visitors at Penrhyn, 1866. The group includes the Archbishop of Canterbury and Mrs Tait, Col. Douglas-Pennant (in the top hat), Mr and Mrs Liddell, Mrs W. E. Gladstone (seated centre right), Mr Herbert Gladstone, the Hon. Edward and Mrs Douglas, and the Hon. C. Hanbury Tracy

(Opposite page) Edward Douglas-Pennant, 1st Baron Penrhyn (1800–86); painting by Eden Eddis (No.68, Dining Room)

they spent a few nights at Penrhyn. Mr Gladstone enjoyed himself very much, despite having to submit to being weighed – 11 st. 10½ lbs – and measured – 5 ft 11 in. in his shoes – by Col. Douglas-Pennant's daughters.

More remarkable was Col. Douglas-Pennant's friendship with prominent local politicians such as John Morgan, owner of a small factory at Cadnant, a Welsh radical and editor of a Welsh newspaper whose opinions Adela Douglas-Pennant described as 'advanced'. Her father was prominent in public works: he gave land for schools and churches, improved the Bangor infirmary, and contributed to the restoration of Bangor Cathedral. His restoration of the parish church at Llandygai may have had more to do with landscape improvements, since the tower became a feature in the principal distant views of the castle.

When Col. Douglas-Pennant was raised to the peerage in 1866, his son, George Sholto, succeeded him as MP for Carnarvonshire. When the seat was next contested, in 1868, George Sholto was defeated by W. J. Parry, a Liberal, the son of a Bethesda quarryman but himself a young professional with diverse business interests. This event is perhaps symbolic of the passing not only of an era in Caernarfonshire politics but of the old order of the paternalistic landlord in the county.

George Sholto Douglas-Pennant was born in 1836 and educated at Oxford. As a young man he travelled in Egypt, Syria, the Holy Land and the Balkans, and in America he is said to have witnessed Blondin's tightrope walk across Niagara. Returning from his travels in 1860 he married Pamela Rushout, daughter of Sir Charles Rushout of Sezincote in Gloucestershire. She bore him seven children, and they were a devoted couple. Her death only nine years after their marriage threw him into a decline, which was only arrested by two further years abroad in the early 1870s, collecting curiosities and corresponding regularly with his young family. In 1875 his recovery was completed by his marriage to Gertrude Jessy Glynne, a niece of Mrs Gladstone; Jessy is said to have reminded him of his first wife.

George Sholto succeeded as 2nd Baron Penrhyn on his father's death in 1886. He had assumed the ownership of the quarry a year earlier, and his reign

George Sholto Douglas-Pennant, 2nd Lord Penrhyn (1836–1907); painting by Barbara Leighton (No.231, Dining Room)

is chiefly remembered for the great strike of 1900–3 (see Chapter Eight). The 2nd Baron maintained an interest in archaeology throughout his life, probably acquiring for the castle both the Egyptian artefacts on display, the 'Book of the Dead' papyrus and the stone figure of Osiris. He subscribed to the publications of his first cousin Augustus Lane-Fox (later known as General Pitt-Rivers), and was also a keen naturalist. His patronage of the firm of Morris and Co., whose wallpapers and fabrics were ordered for the Keep bedrooms in the 1890s, reveals another facet of his complex personality.

The numerous racing trophies in the castle are evidence of the 2nd Baron's success as a breeder and trainer of racehorses, both at Penrhyn and at Exton in Lincolnshire. Like his father and his son he was an active Master of the Grafton Hunt, but as *Bailey's Monthly Magazine of Sports and Pastimes* reported in 1888:

Fond as he is of silk and scarlet, he is, perhaps, more devoted to his 'rod' than any other sport, for in early spring and late autumn he never fails to spend a few weeks on Dee side, and until he succeeded to the cares as well as the houses of the title and estate, he was an annual visitor to Norway... The 12th finds him on his Welsh moors, whence nothing can lure him till the saddling bell at Doncaster sends forth its Leger clang.

Lord Penrhyn's family was large and spread over a wide range of ages. Among the daughters of his first marriage were the artistically inclined Alice, who published a catalogue of the family pictures in 1902, and was renowned for her prowess at skating, and at swimming in Samuel Wyatt's Marine Bath; Hilda, a close friend of Lady Ottoline Morrell; and

The 2nd Lord Penrhyn, Lady Penrhyn, and the future 3rd Baron

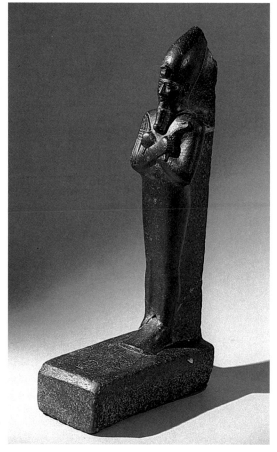

Granite figure of Osiris (Dining Room). It may have been acquired by the 2nd Baron, who took a keen interest in archaeology

Violet, who worked as First Insurance Commissioner for Wales under Lloyd George, and later commanded the WRAF during the Second World War.

When the 2nd Baron died in 1907, he was succeeded to all his estates by his eldest son, Edward Sholto Douglas-Pennant, 3rd Lord Penrhyn. He had met his wife, Hon. Blanche Fitzroy, at Wicken, and as an asthmatic she greatly preferred the climate there to the maritime air at Penrhyn. Edward Sholto was MP for Southern Northamptonshire from 1895 to 1900, and subsequently spent some time living at Glan Conway, the house his grandfather had bought as a shooting lodge on the Ysbyty Ifan estate.

In the First World War, Lord Penrhyn's eldest son and heir, Alan George Sholto Douglas-Pennant, and his two half brothers – children of his father's second marriage – George and Charles, were all killed in action. After the war, Lord Penrhyn lived at Wicken, which he left to his widow on his death in 1927.

33

His only surviving son, Hugh Napier Douglas-Pennant, succeeded him as 4th Baron. In 1922 he had married Hon. Sybil Mary, daughter of the 3rd Viscount Hardinge (the marriage was dissolved in 1941, and Lady Penrhyn later remarried). She was a cousin of the Hon. C. S. Rolls, and it was at her instigation that in 1936 Lord Penrhyn acquired the Rolls-Royce that still belongs to the family. Their time at Penrhyn is remembered as a golden age of entertaining and weekend house-parties. Although they had no children, the many grandchildren of the 3rd Baron were frequent visitors, and Lady Penrhyn furnished the rooms with comfortable sofas and cut flowers to overcome the exaggerated formality of the Victorian age. Lord Penrhyn was Lord Lieutenant of Carnarvonshire from 1933 to 1941.

Like many other country houses, Penrhyn was pressed into unlikely service during the Second World War. On 23 August 1939, after months of careful preparation, the National Gallery's collection of Old Masters was evacuated from London to Aberystwyth, Bangor and Penrhyn to be beyond the range of enemy bombers. Penrhyn was chosen because it was one of the few buildings in Wales with doors large enough to admit the biggest of the National Gallery's paintings, Van Dyck's equestrian portrait of Charles I. The pictures were stored in the

(Above) Edward Sholto, 3rd Lord Penrhyn (1864–1927) at Penrhyn

(Left) Van Dyck's equestrian portrait of Charles I being unloaded in the Stables. Old Masters from the National Gallery in London were briefly stored at Penrhyn during the Second World War

The Drawing Room became an office for the Daimler motor company from 1940 to 1945

Dining Room and two coach-houses, but this refuge proved only temporary. The fall of France in 1940 increased the threat of bombing, and it was thought safer to move the collection underground to a slate mine at Blaenau Ffestiniog. From 1940 to 1945 the castle was the headquarters of the Daimler motor company. At the same time (1940–3) the BBC's variety department occupied a hall in Bangor built in the 1860s for the coming-of-age of the 2nd Lord Penrhyn. Arthur Askey, Kenneth Horne, and Tommy Handley's *ITMA* were all broadcast from here.

In 1949, the 4th Lord Penrhyn left Penrhyn Castle to his niece, Lady Janet Marcia Rose Harper (*née* Pelham) and the title became separate. Frank Douglas-Pennant, 5th Baron, is noted for having won the 1908 Grand National with the 66–1 outsider, Rubio, which had seen service between the shafts of a hotel omnibus at Towcester, and for having made his maiden speech in the House of Lords at the age of 100 in 1967.

In respect of her uncle's will, Lady Janet and her husband, Mr John Charles Harper, assumed the surname and arms of Douglas Pennant. They lived in Penrhyn for a few months only in 1949, then moved to the agent's house, and subsequently to a new house nearby. In 1951, Penrhyn Castle and the Ysbyty Ifan and Carneddau estates (except for Glan Conway House and two farms) were accepted by the Inland Revenue under the then National Land Fund procedures, and transferred to the National Trust. Lady Janet and her husband continued to be closely involved with the castle and the Trust's work there. Following the death of Lady Janet in 1997, Richard Douglas Pennant, her son, inherited the estate, and, once again in lieu of death duties, the Trust acquired further paintings, furniture and silver gilt.

NOTES

1 *Ein Herbst in Wales*, 1856.
2 Op. cit.

CHAPTER FIVE

THE PICTURES

Penrhyn has been called 'the Gallery of North Wales' and in terms of quality, it certainly deserves that title. The Douglas-Pennant pictures also form a rare intact survival in Britain of a nineteenth-century collection. The family, which still owns the collection, has in recent years generously increased the number and importance of the paintings on loan, so that visitors can enjoy them in the surroundings for which they were originally acquired.

Apart from some earlier family pictures, most of which are portraits, the collection is almost entirely the creation of one man, Col. Edward Gordon Douglas-Pennant, 1st Baron Penrhyn (1800–86). What is more, it was to a considerable extent acquired through the agency and on the advice of one dealer, the Belgian C.J. Nieuwenhuys. It thus has a homogeneity rare in nineteenth-century collections. Indeed Douglas-Pennant appears to have chosen for Penrhyn only paintings whose scale and force of character would enable them to hold their own in the overpowering context of its neo-Norman interiors. This is particularly true of his Dutch pictures; the smaller and lighter works all seem to have been allocated to the family's London home.

This aptness of the pictures to their surroundings at Penrhyn reflects the reputed origin of Col. Douglas-Pennant's activity as a collector. According to some manuscript reminiscences of Adela Douglas-Pennant:

Mr Dawkins-Pennant, besides wishing the property to be extended, had expressly desired that a good collection of pictures should be made at Penrhyn by his heirs, and my Father [Col. Douglas-Pennant] took pains to carry out his wishes. It was a task in accordance with his tastes, for although he had not much time in his youth for the study of art history, he had some talent for sketching, and he was a lover of pictures and no mean judge of them.

What may have begun as a duty imposed, undoubtedly gathered its own momentum. Col. Douglas-Pennant started slowly: although he inherited in 1840, few if any purchases are recorded from that decade. Among the first, assuming that Douglas-Pennant bought it when it was exhibited at the Royal Academy, or shortly thereafter, must have been *St John the Baptist preaching to Herod* (No. 149, Passage to Keep) of 1848 by J.R. Herbert. Herbert was a forerunner of the Pre-Raphaelites, much influenced by the German Nazarenes, who turned to painting religious subjects of this kind after his conversion to Catholicism. That it was an early purchase, in a taste that he subsequently outgrew, is suggested by Alice Douglas-Pennant's terse statement: 'Bought by Edward, Lord Penrhyn (who afterwards disliked it very much).'

In or around 1850, Douglas-Pennant bought his first Old Master, not from a dealer but from his son's tutor, a Mr Scoltock, who had in turn bought it when travelling on the Continent with Lord Ashburton. This was the solitary masterpiece of its kind in the collection, the Dieric Bouts of *St Luke painting the Madonna and Child* (No. 92, Ebony Room), a picture whose quality would be much more evident were it still on panel, and were it not for the losses that it suffered in the transfer to canvas, and before. Some of this damage must be attributable to the fact that 'Lord Penrhyn... never cared for it at all', and that it was among the pictures relegated to the top of the castle. Taken together, the two purchases, with his subsequent reaction against them, suggest that Col. Douglas-Pennant began with a taste for the primitive, whether in its original form or in its revived manifestations, but soon underwent revulsion from this. (He may have turned against the

(Right) 'St Luke painting the Madonna and Child', studio of Dieric Bouts (No.92, Ebony Room)

Herbert on discovering that the artist was a Catholic convert, and against 'primitive' paintings like the Bouts because of similar associations.)

It is dangerous to presume too much from the somewhat random survival of evidence for Col. Douglas-Pennant's purchases, but it would appear that there was a hiatus, and that he did not start collecting again until 1855, when he made three or four purchases, all of Old Masters, and all from Nieuwenhuys. There are even indications that it was only once he had acquired Nieuwenhuys, not simply as a dealer but as a mentor, that he began to collect paintings in earnest. Nieuwenhuys's letters to Col. Douglas-Pennant detailing what had been bought sound more than mere dealer's patter; they convey the trusted advice of a man who, bred in the business of buying and selling paintings, and moving freely between the art worlds of Brussels, Paris, London and Amsterdam, simply had a breadth of experience to which Col. Douglas-Pennant could not aspire, and to which he naturally deferred.

'Catrina Hooghsaet',
by Rembrandt (No.19,
Breakfast Room)

Christianus Johannes Nieuwenhuys (1799–1883) was the son of a Netherlandish dealer active in Paris, who seems quickly to have seen that the future lay in England. One of his earliest successes was the sale of Correggio's *Madonna of the Basket* to the newly founded National Gallery in 1825. In 1834 he published *A Review of the Lives and Works of some of the most Eminent Painters*, partly puffing his own activities; and in 1837 and 1843, catalogues of the collection of King Willem II of Holland. He was a substantial buyer at the Northwick Park sale in 1859, and he seems to have had a hand in forming the Beaucousin Collection which was bought *en bloc* by the National Gallery in 1860. Little is known of his private life, other than that he married his niece in 1826, who died after only three months' marriage, and had remarried by 1856. He lived latterly at Oxford Lodge, Wimbledon, and Adela Douglas-Pennant recorded that 'many times did we drive there with my Father to inspect any treasures discovered by the old man at sales'.

The concentration of Lord Penrhyn's collection on just a few categories of picture strongly suggest that, once he had started collecting in earnest, he was sure of his own taste. There appear to have been three kinds of picture that primarily appealed to him: Dutch seventeenth-century, with a particular partiality for large landscapes and dignified figural subjects; Venetian sixteenth-century conversation-pieces; and Spanish seventeenth-century, with an especial predilection for somewhat austere portraiture (Col. Douglas-Pennant had served in Portugal and visited Spain as a young man). Otherwise – with the signal exception of the Rembrandt (No. 19, Breakfast Room) – portraiture seems to have interested him but moderately, despite the fact that both his favourite Dutch and Venetians were amongst its supreme exponents. There is no Frans Hals, for instance, and his relatively cheaply acquired Tintoretto was kept at his London house. There was good reason for this, in that – in addition to the usual accumulations of family portraits – the castle contained a number of portraits of historical personages bought by its builder, George Dawkins-Pennant – some of them at the sale of Lord Charles Townshend in 1819.

It was exceptional, subsequent to the Herbert, for Col. Douglas-Pennant to buy anything from a

F. R. Lee painted 'The River Ogwen at Cochwillan Mill' (No.111, Grand Hall Gallery) while staying at Penrhyn

The Dining Room, hung with Colonel Douglas-Pennant's Spanish, Italian and English pictures, c.1900

contemporary artist. A Creswick (not shown), a Frederick Lee (No. 111, Grand Hall Gallery), a Clarkson Stanfield (No. 109, Grand Hall Gallery), and three ambitious watercolours by Carl Haag (Nos. 234–6, Keep Bedroom) are about the sum of it (leaving portraits aside again). Even then, personal associations accounted for most of these: the Lee shows the artist fishing, accompanied by a friend of Col. Douglas-Pennant and his Keeper, and was painted when the artist came to stay; the Haags were painted by a protégé of Col. Douglas-Pennant's mentor in matters of watercolour, the eminent surgeon and amateur watercolourist, Sir Prescott Hewett Bt (1812–91). The Stanfield, now sadly ruined, is itself an interesting illustration of the recidivism of his taste, bought as it was in the 1870s. For Stanfield was one of those artists initially praised to the skies by Ruskin, but later condemned by him as meretricious, once Turner had opened his eyes to the true observation of Nature and natural effects, and the Pre-Raphaelites had chimed with his aspirations for moral renewal through art.

According to Alice Douglas-Pennant, whose privately printed catalogue is almost the only source of information that we have on many of the pictures, Col. Douglas-Pennant was constantly changing the arrangement of his pictures. This was mostly to accommodate new purchases, but he also relegated all the earlier accumulations of pictures to the upper floors, and housed his own in the two Dining Rooms, and in his own and Lady Penrhyn's Sitting Rooms. A major rationalisation took place in 1899, when the 2nd Lord Penrhyn had the pictures all restored and cleaned, taking the opportunity to rehang them by School – Spanish, Italian and English in the Dining Room; and Dutch primarily in the Breakfast Room. This (like Alice Douglas-Pennant's catalogue) was under the direction of Sir Walter Armstrong, who, as Director of the National Gallery, might be expected to countenance this somewhat unusual rationalisation for a private house. But Penrhyn has been open to the public since its earliest days, so perhaps the survival of some of this didacticism in the present arrangement is not inappropriate.

CHAPTER SIX
THE CASTLE

THE CARRIAGE FORECOURT

The view over the parapet of the Carriage Forecourt must have decided Hopper and his patron in favour of placing the main entrance on this side of the castle, although both earlier houses on the site had been approached from the west, or opposite, side.

The two eminences in the distance are the Great and Little Orme, with the isthmus of Llandudno in between. Along the coast are the headlands of Penmaenmawr and Penmaenbach, and the high plateau of the Carneddau, with the peaks of Carnedd Dafydd and Carnedd Llywelyn to the right. Further round, just out of sight in the cleft in the mountains, lurks the mighty Penrhyn slate quarry. Away to the left (north east) is Puffin Island (Priestholm), lying off the south-eastern tip of Anglesey, opposite the headland of Penmon, the source of the limestone from which the castle is built.

Standing on the Forecourt it is possible to take in the three 'compartments' of the castle's plan. To the south, the great Keep rises to 115 feet, containing the family

The Carriage Forecourt in 1846; lithograph by G. Hawkins

bedrooms and living rooms arranged on four floors. In the centre is the principal block of 'state' rooms, always intended for occasional use, sumptuously furnished and open to the public from the start. To the right is the vast range of domestic, stable and out-offices that kept the castle going, starting with the Housemaids' Tower and ranging beyond the high curtain wall of the stables.

Above the entrance are the crests of the Dawkins and Pennant families: *Out of a ducal coronet an antelope's head tufted, horned and crined* and *A dexter arm embowed ensigned with a crescent holding a battle-axe blade charged with a rose*.

THE ENTRANCE GALLERY

This was one of the later parts of the principal block of the castle to be built, the foundations starting in 1829, by which time the Keep was being roofed. The great oak door, with its carved surround, may not have been fitted until as late as 1835.

Inside the narrow, low Entrance Gallery the impression is of a Norman cloister, clearly designed to accentuate the impact of the Grand Hall beyond, which is partly hidden from view by the deliberate offsetting of the doorways in between.

FURNITURE AND METALWORK

Along the Gallery and vestibule are several of Hopper's neo-Norman carved oak tables and desks made by the estate carpenters; early eighteenth-century Flemish armchairs with carved cherub heads to the arms; some 'ancient' hall chairs probably made to Hopper's order and based on a late-sixteenth-century German pattern book; and two oak hall chairs with double-headed eagles carved in the oval backs and dated 1729 (probably made up in the 1830s by Hopper).

The most bizarre piece is a high-backed carved oak armchair whose eclectic composition epitomises early nineteenth-century antiquarian taste. The central panel of the back, surrounded by late Seventeenth-century-style decoration, is carved with a standing figure of a crusader. The 'wings' seem indebted to a 'Renaissance' source, the seat and arms are covered in late seventeenth-century embossed leather, and the cabriole legs are of a basically Georgian kind.

The set of four bronzed iron colza-oil lamps on pedestals lost their oil reservoirs with the coming of electricity. Their wolf-heads may have been derived from the antique Capitoline Wolf bronze in Rome.

PHOTOGRAPH

Hanging behind the desk is a photograph taken outside the front door during the visit of the Prince and Princess of Wales in July 1894. The Princess is seated in the centre, with the Prince standing to her left. Lady Penrhyn is seated to the right of the Princess; her husband, the 2nd Lord Penrhyn, is the bearded figure standing behind.

THE GRAND HALL

At a point just beyond the door from the vestibule to the Hall the two main axes of the plan cross, and all three 'compartments' of the castle are within view. To the left, up a flight of steps, lie the family sitting-rooms in the Keep. Probably in the time of the 1st Lord Penrhyn an outside door was let into the west of this passage to enable him to slip out without notice, often to the Ogwen River with his rod. To the right, the door at the far end of the corridor marks the boundary between the principal rooms and the domestic offices. Straight ahead is the vast empty volume of the Grand Hall, the *atrium* as it were, of the castle, as much a covered courtyard as a room, and, as one writer has put it, 'about as homely as a great railway terminus ... admirably suited to house an exhibition of locomotives, or outsize dinosaurs' (Hague 1959, p.43). Though it may resemble the nave or transept of a cathedral, no direct source exists, and the compound arches of the 'clerestory' are particularly unusual.

The floor here (and in the adjacent passages and stairs) is of York stone, specified by Hopper on the strength of its recent use at Westminster Hall and York Minster.

PICTURES

Listed numerically within each room, the numbers deriving from Alice Douglas-Pennant's 1902 catalogue.

133 Attributed to ISAAC SEEMAN (fl.1720–51)
? John Pennant (d.1781)
The pendant to No.134, Grand Hall (aisles), and can therefore be dated to 1749. (See No.49 for biography.)

IN THE PASSAGE TO THE KEEP:

47 ENGLISH (eighteenth century)
Sir Samuel Pennant (1709–50)
Son of Edward Pennant of Jamaica; younger brother of No.49. Apparently by the same hand as No.49; and possibly Nos.133 and 134. For another portrait see No.134.

The Grand Hall in 1846, showing the frontispiece to the fireplace, since removed; lithograph by G. Hawkins

49 ENGLISH (eighteenth century)
? John Pennant (d.1781)
Son of Edward Pennant of Jamaica; elder brother of
No.47; father of No.58, Dining Room. He became a
successful Liverpool merchant and also acquired his
younger brother Henry's Jamaican property as a lifetime gift in 1761, having previously succeeded to his
share of Samuel's. For related pictures see No.47.

97 ENGLISH (seventeenth century)
Sir Robert Williams, 2nd Bt (c.1629–80)
Married a daughter of Sir John Glynne (No.48, Dining
Room).

149 JOHN ROGERS HERBERT, RA (1810–90)
John the Baptist Preaching to Herod
Signed and dated 1848
Exhibited at the Royal Academy, 1848. Bought by
Edward 1st Lord Penrhyn who 'afterwards disliked it
very much'. Although seemingly Pre-Raphaelite, and
indeed exhibited in the year that the Brotherhood was
founded, this picture actually belongs to an earlier
strain of retrospective, religious painting influenced
by the German Nazarenes. Herbert had begun by
painting colourful scenes of Italian life and history,
but after his conversion to Roman Catholicism by
Pugin around 1841, turned to religious subjects such
as this.

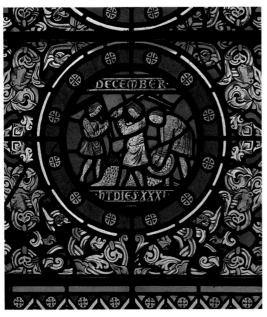

*Detail from the Grand Hall stained glass by Thomas
Willement*

On a table to one side is the first of the series of
lithographs of Penrhyn by G. Hawkins, published in
1846. The massive frontispiece to the fireplace seems
to have been dismantled early this century, as it
prevented the fire from drawing properly, but the
luminaires shown in the print remain. Their sculptural
bases are made from an unidentified ceramic successor
of Coade stone and the lamps themselves have unusually large oil reservoirs. Their maker is not known.

STAINED GLASS
The stained glass was all supplied in 1835–6 by Thomas
Willement, who travelled from London in July 1834
'to see the situation of the Hall windows'. The two
largest, at the northern end, are signed by him and
dated 1835. They are among his best work, incorporating the signs of the zodiac alternating with
roundels illustrating the months of the year, in a
convincing thirteenth-century style reminiscent of
windows at Canterbury Cathedral.

In the vault above the main space of the Hall, his
four skylights are actually set some 15 feet below the
roof, and the light 'borrowed' by means of lath and
plaster 'funnels' rising through the roof space.

CLOCK
The clock above the fireplace is by William Johnson,
'50 Strand, London, 1835' and the accompanying
wind direction dial is linked to a vane on the roof.

FURNITURE
The large octagonal carved oak tilt-top table was
designed by Hopper and incorporates fragments
from earlier furniture in the pedestal base. His start-
lingly original design for the oak chairs, with backs
carved like the vanes of some marine organism, was
never imitated. They are surprisingly comfortable
and give excellent support to the back. The settees in
the window embrasures came more recently from
a London Club. The piano is an iron-framed Broad-
wood concert grand in a rosewood case, No.47778,
1903.

TEXTILES
The machine-woven Axminster 'Turkey' runner was
made in 1987, reproducing the hand-knotted carpet in
the Keep passage, which is probably late nineteenth-
century. The spectacular stamped woollen velvet
curtains date from the early 1830s.

The Library in 1846; lithograph by Hawkins

THE LIBRARY

This extraordinary room partly incorporates the area of the medieval house, of which the solar or 'withdrawing' wing occupied the space to the right of the dividing arcade, and this may have suggested the historical emphasis of the decoration. The flattened form of the three main arches resembles that of the Norman chancel arch at Tickencote church, Leicestershire, which had been rebuilt in the 1790s and included in Carter's *Ancient Architecture* of 1798. The ornament, however, differed.

The decoration and furnishing are almost unchanged since 1846, when this room was depicted in a Hawkins lithograph, which can be seen on a table by the door from the Hall. The decoration of the four arches dividing the room, which included some of the most gruesome animal masks in the castle, had become intolerable by the 1930s and was removed. The ceiling appears originally to have been wood-grained;

Hopper delighted in the sort of trickery achieved by making different materials appear the same in juxtaposition.

CEILING BOSSES

Dawkins-Pennant's heraldic programme for the castle seems to have sprung from a desire to express ancient title to his property. The principal ceiling bosses in line from the Grand Hall doorway bear the components of his coat-of-arms:

1 Sir Gruffydd Llwyd, Bart; 2 Dawkins and Pennant; 3 Yonas ap Goronwy.

Those on the other side of the dividing arcade denote:

4 Yswitan Wyddel; 5 Dawkins and Pennant.

At the lesser intersections are devices of the Dawkins, Pennant and Bouverie families.

STAINED GLASS

Probably the work of David Evans of Shrewsbury, who was paid £7 6s for stained glass in 1836, it shows the arms of the five 'royal' and fifteen 'noble' tribes of Wales, groupings first made at the end of the fifteenth century by the bards – with little reference to historical fact – and taken up by the eighteenth-century antiquaries.

CHIMNEY-PIECES

The four chimney-pieces are of polished Penmon limestone ('Penmon marble') laid down on Anglesey 345 million years ago. The capitals of one of them are carved with two friezes of mummers, taken from the marginalia of a fourteenth-century Bruges manuscript, as illustrated in Joseph Strutt's *Sports and Pastimes* (1801). This choice of subject suggests that the Library was intended not only as the evening resort of gentlemen but as a setting for family entertainments. High Victorian Penrhyn obviously witnessed such productions; for an inventory of 1928 lists 'Theatrical Equipment' among the croquet sets languishing in an upper passage. But the Library must chiefly be thought of as the gentleman's domain, resembling as it does a London club.

BOOKCASES

Examples of bookcases in the form of classical temples can be found in other houses, and Hopper, freed from the constraint of actual Norman precedent, seems here to have translated this idea into the 'Norman' language. The gilt brass grilles were made by a Mr Harris of Wardour St in London, who began them in July 1834 and was paid in February the following year. For making the 2,917 'square ornaments' at the intersections he received £48 12s 4d.

Most of the books date from the time of Richard Pennant and his two successors, although there are earlier volumes that may have been acquired by previous generations. As it survives today, the collection has a good representation of topography, history, architecture and antiquities.

OTHER FURNITURE

The room contains a mixture of contemporary, 'ancient' and composite furniture. Contemporary are the circular table on a tripod stand, veneered in coromandel wood and inlaid with brass, the pole-screens with embroideries by Charlotte Douglas, sister of the 1st Lord Penrhyn, and the seat furniture upholstered in stamped wool velvets. These velvets were produced in the 1820s–'50s in Britain and the Netherlands, on embossed rollers, the designs taken from sixteenth- and seventeenth-century Italian models. The prie-dieu chair is covered in a cut velvet directly reproducing a seventeenth-century Italian design.

Those pieces which may have been bought as 'ancient' include the eighteenth-century 'Burgomaster' chair from the Dutch East Indies, of a type illustrated in Henry Shaw's *Specimens of Ancient Furniture* of 1836 as 'of the time of William the Third', the triangular armchair with an inlaid ivory coronet in the back, of the same origin and date, and the two seventeenth-century Italian high-backed armchairs.

There are several pieces designed by Thomas Hopper and made by the estate carpenters. These are the 'Norman' style square tables with four cluster-column legs, and the octagonal table near the Grand Hall doorway, which incorporates ancient carvings applied to the frieze and column support. In the 1820s and '30s there were many sales of such carvings, some removed from churches, and several London dealers specialised in them. The decoration of the great table at the far end of the Library is also made up from a combination of old carvings with modern work in the same style.

The billiard table may originally have been in the Ebony Room. By 1943 it was at the southern end of the Grand Hall, and was moved to its present position in order to make room for the typing pool of the Daimler Co. Ltd. Unusually, not only the bed, but the entire frame and legs and even the pockets are composed of enamelled slate, and its construction is also thought to be unique. It was made for Col. Douglas-Pennant by George Eugene Magnus, who owned a quarry in North Wales and established the Pimlico Slate Works in London in 1840. Magnus owed his success particularly to developing an enamelling process which produced the high finish visible on this table. The opportunity to demonstrate the versatility of his principal product must have been irresistible to 'Colonel Slate'.

CLOCK

The Boulle-work mantel clock is by Henry Balthazar, Paris, *c*.1740. The base is a nineteenth-century addition.

CARPETS

The carpets at Penrhyn are either luxurious Axminsters based on continental examples or splendid inventions (either by Hopper or Willement) in the Norman style (that is, decorated with 'Norman' patterns, the fitted carpet having been unknown to William the Conqueror). The Library carpets must surely be in their original positions, although their detail differs from that in the lithograph. They are hand-knotted and most probably made at the Axminster factory. The colours, now much faded, were originally yellow ochre, terracotta and brown.

STUFFED BIRDS

The group of exotic birds displayed under a glass dome includes two Indian Rollers (*Coracias bengalensis*; the large birds shown as in flight), some African shrikes (*Lanarius*) and an African mangrove kingfisher (*Halcyon senegaloides*).

SPADE

Leaning against one of the cluster columns is the spade used by the Queen of Romania to plant a tree in the grounds in 1890.

THE DRAWING ROOM

The design of the new castle respected the plan of the medieval house, and this room incorporates the original great hall. From the Library one enters at what was the 'dais' end of the hall, facing the screens passage at the opposite end. The remodelling of this side of the castle is best appreciated by reference to the drawings on the table in the central window bay.

The earlier drawing by Moses Griffith shows, at the top, the western elevation of the medieval house, in which the gable end of the solar wing, now incor-

The Drawing Room

porated in the Library, is shown on the right. Between this wing and the turreted tower (the subject of a licence of 1433 to build 'a little turret with a little battlement') is the hall now displaced by the Drawing Room.

The lower drawing shows the buildings that stood almost opposite this west front, flanking an entrance to the stables. To the right of the arch is the east window of the fifteenth-century chapel, re-erected further to the north west in the 1780s. To the left of the arch were the steward's office and muniment room.

The other coloured drawing is a crude copy, made in 1821, of Moses Griffith's 1806 view of the Wyatt house from the south west (National Library of Wales, Aberystwyth). The protruding square block to the right was a later modification to the design, and seems to foreshadow the present Keep. Also on the table is another of G. Hawkins's lithographs, showing this room in 1846.

DECORATION

The Drawing Room was the domain of the ladies. Its dazzling silk hangings, Curtains and upholstery may have been supplied by one Shales who is mentioned in a letter from Hopper to his client in 1830. By the 1930s the fabrics had probably perished to an extent that they had to be removed, and for much of this century the walls have been covered by a dull brown paint. Probably also in the 1930s, the ceiling was painted over in white and the carved woodwork was stripped of its polish.

In 1985 the silk lampas (often called brocade) was rewoven especially for the room by Prelle et Cie. of Lyon, copying a fragment of the old fabric found on the massive settee beneath later coverings. At the same time the silk tape for binding the curtains and wall hangings, the silk rope and gimp for the upholstery, and the glazed woollen 'tammy' lining for the curtains were reproduced in England from original fragments. Since it was not possible to remove the paint to uncover the 2,000 gilt crosses that appear in the lithograph, these had to be reapplied on top of the original ones. At the same time, the carved woodwork was revived and repolished; the unusual pelmets in the form of outsize curtain poles, and the pulleys and rails themselves, were all made by the castle's own craftsmen. The castle carpenter also made a replacement panel for the back of one of the doors, where china shelves had been set up in the early part of this century.

STAINED GLASS

The medieval hall had been the work of Gwilym ap Gruffydd II and his wife Joan, and Thomas Pennant tells us that their arms could be seen in the windows

until 1764. As an echo of this arrangement, Dawkins-Pennant set up his own arms (impaling those of Elizabeth Bouverie, his second wife) over the central window. This glass and the heraldic windows to either side are attributed to David Evans of Shrewsbury.

CHIMNEY-PIECE

The chimney-piece is of serpentinite, an igneous rock properly called Mona Marble, and this colour occurs in Llanfechell and Llandyfriog on Anglesey.

FURNITURE

Catherine Sinclair noticed 'the largest mirror ever made in this country', and also an organ 'fit for a cathedral ...' here in 1833. The organ was probably identical to the one in Llandygai church, whose dimensions exactly fit the spaces now occupied by the mirrors. (One local tradition asserts that the Drawing Room organ was later plundered for parts to repair the church instrument.) That Miss Sinclair refers to only

The carved and gilt wood leg of one of the Drawing Room tables

one outsize mirror seems to confirm that the organ was at one end; it had been removed and replaced with a matching mirror by 1846, when it was not shown in the lithograph of the room.

Below the mirrors at either end is a pair of highly individual tables*. The one against the Library wall is made entirely of slate, carved exceptionally deeply for this material, and the top slab incorporates 'sample' squares of colourful stones, probably all from Anglesey: in the three larger panels are the two varieties of Mona Marble, the red one as used in the chimneypiece, and the green from Holy Island. At the far end of the room the stand of the other table has the same design of entwined fishes and serpents, but in carved and gilt wood. The top is inlaid with brass stringing. These tables were presumably designed by Hopper, but their makers are not known. If the organ was originally placed at one end, one of the tables must be slightly later than the other.

The massive oak settee, in what might be called the 'Tudor style', the carved oak chairs and the smaller settee (with ancient carving applied to the back and apron) were all designed by Hopper.

The octagonal table with marquetry in the frieze and tripod stand is by Edward Holmes Baldock. Baldock may also have 'made up' the oval table with an 'oyster' marquetry top on a seventeenth-century marquetry stand, and the sixteen-sided marquetry-topped table.

The set of oak 'occasional' chairs of slender Gothic design bears the label of 'James Hughes, Upholsterer, Carnarvon, Late of S.J. Waring and Sons Ltd'. The prie-dieu chair is stamped by Miles and Edwards, London furniture makers and dealers in fabrics. Its serial number indicates that it was supplied after 1833. The table with the drawings and lithographs on it is another 'made-up' piece, incorporating eighteenth-century Dutch inlays and cruder 1830s ones.

CLOCK

The 14-day striking bracket clock in a Boulle-work case is by Jean le Dieux, Paris, c.1700.

CARPET

The carpet is of English manufacture, c.1830, from an earlier Savonnerie design.

METALWORK

The tall gilt-bronze candelabra at either end of the room are traditionally said to be based on an original by the sixteenth-century Italian goldsmith Benvenuto Cellini, but there is no precedent for them in his work. The figures of the seated satyr and the young man with

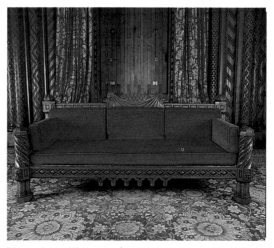
Hopper's neo-Norman oak settee

a syrinx (or pipe) are after the antique marble group of Pan and Daphnis, and the striding figures of satyrs in the upper reaches are also after the Antique. The structure and decorative motifs show a strong Venetian influence, and it is possible that they are the work of a Venetian art foundry of the 1840s.

The two Empire bronze lamps on the mantelpiece, in the form of seated classical female figures, with ormolu mounts and polished granite bases, have been adapted for electricity. Their original form as oil lamps can be seen in Hawkins's print.

CERAMICS

The biscuit porcelain figures and table ornaments are from parts of two Minton dessert services, c.1850, one of them copied from the celebrated eighteenth-century 'Cameo' service made at Sèvres for Catherine the Great.

THE EBONY ROOM

In the doorway between the Drawing Room and the Ebony Room is a door to the spiral stair contained within the medieval tower built by Gwilym ap Gruffydd II, which was retained in Wyatt and Hopper's structures. This part of the present castle, the Oak Tower, is the most complex, probably because much of the two earlier houses was preserved within it.

The unusual ceiling height (a 'mezzanine' room was added above) and the form of the window suggest that this may have been intended as an entrance to the present castle. A much copied engraving, the original of which seems to be that published around 1860 by Catherall, shows this arrangement, with Samuel Wyatt's carriage drive retained to form the approach to an entrance in this position. Since the present eastern Entrance Gallery, barbican and forecourt were all on the undated ground plan (presumed to be by Hopper) and are shown in Hawkins's lithograph of 1846, it remains unclear whether Catherall's print and its progeny were accurate views. The curious alcove in the right-hand wall of the Ebony Room, fitted with a mirror glass, would have made an opening into the Drawing Room which, if this had originally been intended to continue as a great hall, would have resembled the 'screens' opening of the original house, though displaced to the other side of the tower. The mirrored alcove in the opposite wall may mark the position of an earlier, external door to the northern service wing of the medieval house. Whether these additions represent a change of mind in the middle of building is not clear, but it is not impossible that Hopper intended by these devices to give the impression that the room had been remodelled, thus imparting an air of antiquity where none existed.

Here again different materials are used in disguise, and painted and varnished plaster and polished black limestone in the chimney-piece (from Dinorben near Abergele, or Moelfre on Anglesey) complement the furniture, some of which is in solid ebony, some veneered in ebony, and some of other woods, ebonised to give the same effect.

Marked as the 'Boudoir' on the earliest plan, the Ebony Room was presumably the morning room where Mrs Dawkins-Pennant and successive Ladies Penrhyn would work at correspondence and household business, and it was here that Alice Douglas-Pennant compiled her catalogue of the pictures, published in 1902.

PICTURE

92 ? Studio of DIERIC BOUTS (d.1475)
Virgin and Child with St Luke
Transferred from panel to canvas in 1899
The composition is derived from Rogier van der Weyden's (1400–64) treatment of this subject, and ultimately from Jan van Eyck's (active 1422, died 1441) *Virgin and Child with Chancellor Rolin* in the Louvre.

The 1902 catalogue reveals that 'No.92 was bought about 1850 by Edward, Lord Penrhyn, from Mr Scoltock (tutor of his sons), who had bought it whilst travelling abroad with the late Lord Ashburton. Lord Penrhyn gave about £100 or £150 for it, and never cared for it at all. In 1899, being in a bad state, it was found necessary to transfer it from panel to canvas, when it was discovered that the picture had been much

The Ebony Room

A detail of the rich velvet curtains made c.1695–1712

repaired some time ago, several white patches appearing where the paint had been restored, but the heads and figures and all the important parts of the picture were intact.

Legend had it that St Luke painted the Virgin, and hence he is the patron saint of painters and of their guilds and academics. He is shown here making a preliminary drawing in silverpoint, as a contemporary artist would have done. His painted panel stands on an easel in his painting-room on the right of the picture.

FURNITURE

The fashion for ebony furniture of the kind found in this room had been started by Horace Walpole and by 1825 it was becoming essential for any house built in an old English style. Chairs such as the two low examples (not children's chairs) and the taller single chairs (with legs altered in the 1830s) are probably late-eighteenth-century and may have come from Ceylon, but in Britain they were often supplied by dealers as 'ancient', possibly Tudor. The armchairs are of a less exotic style and were probably made in Ceylon in the early nineteenth century specifically for export. The settee may have been made from a design published in Richard Brown's *The Rudiments of Carving Cabinet Furniture and Upholstery* in 1822.

The small cabinet with ivory-inlaid ebony veneer is an older piece, possibly seventeenth-century, from Sindh in India, and the large ebony-veneered *armoire* is Dutch, of the same period. The carved walnut pole-screens were supplied to Col. Douglas-Pennant by C. Hindley and Sons around 1845–6.

TEXTILES

The magnificent green and crimson fabric (originally on a yellow ground) used for the curtains, upholstery and pole-screens is a silk voided *ciselé* velvet in a restrained 'bizarre' design, which dates it between 1695 and 1712. Originally these rich velvets were produced in Genoa, although by this date both Lyon and Spitalfields could have woven such a fabric. How it came to be used here in the 1830s is not clear, but it could have been salvaged from the Warburtons' Cheshire house, Winnington, or bought from a dealer around 1830. (From a letter in the papers of the furniture makers and dealers Miles and Edwards, it appears that Dawkins-Pennant bought old textiles as well as furniture from them.) The provenance of the velvet is all the more intriguing in view of the fact that the much-faded *c.*1830 Lyon silk brocade used for the wall hangings (possibly the silk supplied by one Fentham referred to by Hopper in a letter of November 1830) reproduces part of the same pattern. It was originally ivory, brown and coral red. The wall brocade could well be a direct copy of the velvet made at Lyon, but the precise relationship between the two fabrics remains obscure.

CARPET

The carpet is Persian, *c.*1900.

THE GRAND STAIRCASE

The short curved passage from the Ebony Room seems to be another example of Hopper's penchant for suggesting the presence of earlier fabric, here perhaps a round tower, where none existed; it also provided his joiners with an opportunity for some impressive work in making the door to what was the Steward's office.

The principal staircase must have presented Hopper with a dilemma: how to design a sufficiently impressive stair for such a vast house and yet keep within the Norman style, when he knew that Norman castles had only spiral stone stairs, which could hardly sustain the pitch of the state rooms. He was also very short of space, having only the courtyard of the medieval house (also the site of Wyatt's staircase) to work with. His solution was to make up for this by an orgy of fantastic carving and the use of two contrasting stones: for the walls an oolitic limestone (possibly the Painswick stone of which large blocks were delivered in the late 1820s); and for the carved pylons, balustrades and newels a grey sandstone, possibly from Lancashire. The treads are the same York sandstone used for paving the Grand Hall and corridors.

CARVING

Most of the abstract motifs can be found in Carter's *Ancient Architecture*, but many carved components must contain an element of individual invention, such as the corbel-masks at the door jambs and the extraordinary row of human hands around the arch from the Staircase Hall to the Drawing Room.

The newel 'crowns' of the third flight are carved with panels of figures derived from Strutt's *Sports and Pastimes*. The activities depicted are hawking, archery, slinging and elements of the joust and the tournament, including 'the attack on the quintain', and a King of Arms carrying the banners of the two principal barons of the tournament. The crowns were removed by Sibyl, Lady Penrhyn, in the 1930s but later reinstated, and these operations probably caused the damage visible on some of them.

LANTERN

The riot of plaster in the D-shaped panels seems to owe more to the Norse vocabulary of interlace and the Great Beast than to Norman sources. The influence of Celtic ornament may also be felt. Above these panels the round skylight with 'column' spokes resembles windows at Helingham and Barfreston churches, near Canterbury, illustrated in Carter's *Ancient Architecture*.

The Grand Staircase

A group of three carved limestone capitals between the windows on the top landing of the Grand Staircase

STAINED GLASS

The stained-glass windows are by Thomas Willement and are listed in his *Concise Account of the Principal Works in Stained Glass* (1840) as having been supplied in 1832.

LAMP BRACKETS

The extraordinary cast-iron lamp brackets, where human arms apparently clasping bows emerge from monstrous mouths, were clearly Hopper's design, but it is not known who made them.

THE STATE BEDROOM

This and the adjoining dressing-room are hung with a late eighteenth-century hand-painted Chinese wall-paper, and share the same bizarre plaster cornice, probably derived from illustrations of Tickencote church in Leicestershire by John Carter. The chimney-piece is of the mottled Penmon limestone.

The State Bedroom

The walnut armoire *dates from the 1830s, but the figure of Pluto was carved in Nuremberg 300 years earlier*

FURNITURE

The carved oak bed, the washstand and the *tables de nuit* flanking the bed are Hopper 'Norman' pieces of the 1830s. The former is hung with silver and blue silk lampas, which is also used for the curtains. The fabric is identical in design, although different in colour, to that used in the Drawing Room. It was rewoven in 1992 by Prelle et Cie to replace the original textiles, which are now too fragile to be shown. Less obviously of the 1830s is the large carved walnut *armoire*; the figure of Pluto is from Nuremberg, *c.*1530, but his consort Persephone was carved much later, presumably in the 1830s when the piece was made. The late-seventeenth-century Dutch walnut cabinet-on-stand was also altered in the nineteenth century. The small circular table with three spiral-twist legs and stretchers is by C. Hindley and Sons and was probably bought by the 1st Lord Penrhyn.

Some of the other pieces are earlier: the unusual English *rocaille* looking-glass, *c.*1725–50, on the window wall is covered with shells and coral fragments, and the writing-table below it, with ebony veneer inlaid with floral marquetry, is Louis XIV, *c.*1690.

The painted mirror in a giltwood frame over the fireplace is a nineteenth-century rococo revival piece, inspired by eighteenth-century Chinese export mirror paintings. On the Louis XIV desk are a mid-nineteenth-century Indian ebony dressing-case and a pair of small seventeenth-century lacquer cabinets made in Japan.

CLOCK

The French 8-day striking mantel clock in a gilt brass and porcelain case is signed by Henry Marc, *c.*1880.

CARPET

The hand-knotted Turkish carpet is nineteenth-century.

CERAMICS

On the shelves in the false doorway to the right of the fireplace is part of a Liverpool (impressed *Herculaneum*) dessert service decorated with thistles in the centre. The washstand set in 'pheasant' pattern is nineteenth-century Copeland Spode, and the other bowl and ewer are from a Minton set decorated in 1894. The Cauldon china tea set was supplied by Mortlocks of Oxford St.

THE GRAND HALL GALLERY

PICTURES

150 ENGLISH, nineteenth-century
Penrhyn Castle from Dologwen

111 FREDERICK RICHARD LEE, RA (1798–1879)
The River Ogwen at Cochwillan Mill
Signed and dated 1849
Commissioned by the 1st Lord Penrhyn. The picture shows the artist bringing a salmon to the net held by a keeper, Robert Buckland. The spectator is General Cartwright, a great friend of Lord Penrhyn.

302 J. OLIVER HARRIS
Penrhyn Castle from the south-west
Signed and dated 1890

5 NATHANIEL HONE (1718–84)
David, Viscount Milsington

6 SIR JOSHUA REYNOLDS (1723–92)
Richard Pennant Esq

138 HENRY PICKERING (1752–90)
Portrait of a Man

FURNITURE

The four Ceylonese ebony chairs are of the same date (*c*.1800) and design as two in the Ebony Room.

PASSAGE TO KEEP

At ground- and first-floor levels there are passages connecting the principal rooms with the family apartments and bedrooms in the Keep; the two further storeys of the Keep were accessible by spiral staircases in two of the corner turrets, one for service use, and one for the family and guests. Visitors today can climb the 128 steps from the first floor to the roof, when there is a steward in attendance.

PICTURES

The three mezzotints after Sir Thomas Lawrence represent *The 2nd Marquess of Londonderry* (1769–1822), in Garter robes, scraped by Charles Turner, *Viscount Lascelles* (1767–1841, uncle of the 1st Lord Penrhyn of Llandegai) and *Thomas Graham, Baron*

*The Grand Hall
Gallery*

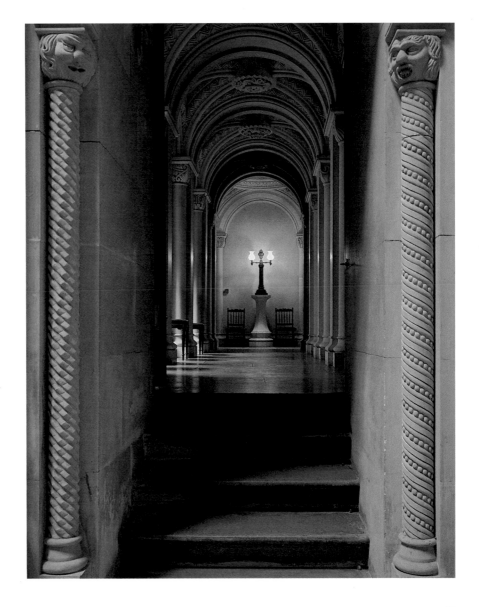

The brass bed was ordered for the Prince of Wales's visit in 1894

Lynedoch (1748–1843). As well as being an outstanding general, Lynedoch is remembered for having played in the first Scottish cricket match, in 1785.

The other prints are of *Lord Petre* by A. Frische after Romney, *Charles James Fox* (1749–1806) by John Jones after Sir Joshua Reynolds, and *Thomas Assheton Smith* (1752–1828) of Vaynol, owner of the rival Dinorwic slate quarry, by S.W. Reynolds after Beechey.

The two colourful West Indian watercolours are valuable records of the appearance of two of the family's Jamaican plantations – *Denbigh* and *Pennants* – by a local artist in 1871. The sugar factory at Denbigh was built by Richard Pennant in 1802 and was still in use in the 1920s, when new machinery was installed by the 3rd Lord Penrhyn.

FURNITURE

The four carved oak side-tables are from Hopper designs and have Mona Marble and Penmon limestone slab tops. The two Ceylonese settees with stamped velvet squabs are early-nineteenth-century in the style of the armchairs in the Ebony Room, but the two single chairs are Victorian.

PICTURES

IN THE PASSAGE TO THE BEDROOMS

151 R.C. (active late eighteenth century)
Six watercolour drawings of scenes in Jamaica
Nothing is known of the history of these drawings, but they are almost certainly connected with the Pennants' Jamaican estates. Alice Douglas-Pennant read the initials found on one of them as 'J.C.', which she interpreted as those of the marine painter, John Clevely, but there is no evidence that he was ever in the West Indies. However, his twin brother Robert (1767–1806), then in the Navy, exhibited a West Indian landscape at the Royal Academy in 1780, and they are possibly by him.

A view of the bridge crossing the River Cobre near Spanish Town

A view of the bridge crossing the Cabaritta River in the parish of Westmoreland

Untitled – A bridge on box piers in a gorge

A prospect of Port Antonio in the parish of Portland

Untitled – A road by a waterfall

Dry Harbour

THE KEEP BEDROOMS

The suite of rooms shown was probably intended as one apartment, to which the passage hung with watercolours (with its baize door) was the staff access. It would have consisted of a sitting-room, a dressing-room, bedroom and a small ante-room. The arrangement is followed in the other storeys of the Keep, and it seems likely that one of these apartments was used by the Queen and Prince Consort during their visit on 15 October 1859. The view from the rooms also accords with George Fripp's drawing, made as a record.

For much of the 2nd Lord Penrhyn's time these rooms were used as, respectively, 'Miss Alice Pennant's Room [now shown as a Nursery: her initials are scratched into one of the window panes], Lord Penrhyn's Bedroom, Gertrude Lady Penrhyn's Room, Young Ladies Sitting Room'.

Unlike the principal rooms, the family rooms in the Keep were redecorated in the late nineteenth century, with wallpapers and fabrics by the firm of Morris & Co. In the first room, probably originally a dressing-room, the paper is Morris, 'Double Bough' of 1890, and the hangings of the bed are made from a woven silk and linen fabric called 'Cross Twigs' designed c.1894, by J. H. Dearle for Morris & Co.

PICTURES

312 WILLIAM HAYES
Eleven studies of birds from 'Mr Child's Menagery' at Osterley Park, Middlesex
Some signed and dated 1785
William Hayes was an impecunious animal painter, who was employed by Robert Child's wife Sarah to portray the inhabitants of her aviary in a series of watercolours which he engraved for publication as *Birds in the Collection of Osterley Park* (1779–86), and *Rare and Curious Birds from Osterley Park* (1794). Richard Pennant may have commissioned similar drawings, but it seems more likely that the Penrhyn series was purchased at the Osterley Park sale in 1885 by George Sholto, 2nd Lord Penrhyn.

FURNITURE

The brass bed was ordered, at a cost of £600, for the use of the Prince of Wales when he stayed at Penrhyn in 1894, but it was probably first set up in a room off the Grand Staircase, and originally had different hangings. The cheval glass and washstand (with a Mona Marble top) are Hopper designs, as is the hand-knotted Axminster carpet, which preserves its original colours better than any of the other 'Norman' examples in the castle.

CERAMICS

A pair of *Dehan blanc-de-Chine* dogs of Fo, *Kangxi*.
A nineteenth-century Chinese *famille rose* trumpet-necked vase.
A Minton toilet set of 'bamboo' design, c.1860–70.

THE SLATE BED

The next bedroom has one of Penrhyn's most famous curiosities. The slate bed* was probably carved by someone who normally produced slate headstones and chest tombs, a peculiarly Welsh tradition of which good examples are to be found in Llandygai churchyard. This bed, and another in the same material, were originally in what were called the Upper and Lower Slate Bedrooms in the north-east corner of the main block of the castle (not open). Iris hung with a printed cotton called 'Pomegranate', designed by William Morris in 1877.

The wallpaper is not by Morris and is probably Edwardian.

The chimney-piece, one of the most spectacular in the castle, is made of the red Mona Marble; the two candlesticks are of the same material, which was also used for the tops of the 'Norman' *tables de nuit*.

PICTURES

109 CLARKSON STANFIELD, RA (1793–1867)
Amalfi: birthplace of the mariner's compass
Stanfield was one of the most successful early Victorian landscape painters. Ruskin called him 'the leader of the English Realists', chided him for being 'somewhat over prosaic', but praised his 'true, salt, serviceable, unsentimental sea'. However, this picture invoked Ruskin's wrath, when shown at the 1848 Royal Academy: 'The lost sentiment of Mr Stanfield's 'Amalfi' – the chief landscape of the year – full of exalted [?] material, and mighty crags, and massy seas, grottos, precipices, and convents; fortress-towers, and cloud-capped mountains – and all in vain, merely because that same simple secret ha, been despised; because nothing there is painted – as it Is ...' (*Modern Painters*, Addenda to Part III, 1848). The picture has suffered badly from the artist's use of bitumen to produce rich, transparent darks. It was bought by the 1st Lord Penrhyn in the 1870s.

The photographs show members of the 1st and 2nd Barons' families.

FURNITURE AND CERAMICS

The seat furniture is upholstered in what must have been a dazzling green silk fabric of the 1890s. Several Hopper-designed pieces include the dressing-table and dressing-mirror, the massive wardrobe with arcaded front, and the washstand. There are two washstand sets: the 12-piece set in blue with gold flower and bird decoration is by Spode, Copeland and Garret, and the part-set in white with pink roses is by Coalport, supplied by T. Goode of London.

BATHROOM

The wallpaper is 'Willow Bough', designed by Morris in 1887. The fittings are Shanks's 'Fin de Siècle' models.

THE ANTE-ROOM

The ante-room adjoining the Bedroom has another Morris wallpaper, 'Iris', designed by J.H. Dearle c.1887, and a Mona Marble chimney-piece.

PICTURES

227 GEORGE FENNEL ROBSON (1790–1833)
*Eight Views of Caernarfonshire and one of Durham**
These watercolours were probably painted for George Hay Dawkins-Pennant, since all but one show views of his Caernarfonshire estates. He probably commissioned the set of eight, and the artist may have added the view of his own birthplace, Durham, in gratitude for such a major commission. They illustrate one of the aims of the Old Watercolour Society, of which Robson was one of the most active members, to put watercolours on a par with oils as gallery pictures.

TO THE LEFT OF THE CHIMNEY-PIECE:
*Penmaenmawr from the grounds of Penrhyn Castle**
*View from the grounds of Penrhyn Castle looking towards Nant Ffrancon**

OVER THE CHIMNEY-PIECE:
*Durham Cathedral and Town**

TO THE LEFT OF THE DOOR:
(ABOVE)
*Moel Tryfan from the south end of Llyn Ogwen**
(BELOW)
*Llyn Idwal**

OVER THE DOOR:
*Carnedd Llywelyn and Carnedd Dafydd**

TO THE RIGHT OF THE DOOR:
(ABOVE)
*Llyn Ogwen from the south**
(BELOW)
*Snowdon from Capel Curig**

FURNITURE

Two Hopper dressing-tables and a *table de nuit**.
An 1830s carved walnut *armoire* in the seventeenth-century Swiss style.
A Regency rosewood teapoy inlaid overall with brass.
An American treadle sewing-machine by Wheeler and Wilson, 1867.
An armchair upholstered in William Morris's 'Windrush' block-printed cotton produced in 1883, now much faded.

PICTURE

GEORGE FENNEL ROBSON (1790–1833)
Penrhyn Castle from Lonisa

THE LOWER INDIA ROOM

Well into the nineteenth century the term 'India' was used to denote anything from the Orient. Here it refers to the Chinese hand-painted wallpaper, which probably dates from c.1800, and would have been set up here in the 1830s. This room was used by the last Lord Penrhyn to live at the castle, Hugh Napier, 4th Baron (1894–1949).

Although their doors have been removed, the positions of the bath and the water-closet in the ante-lobby seem somewhat public. 'The principles of English delicacy are not easily satisfied', wrote Robert Kerr on this subject in his classic *The Gentleman's House* of 1865; '... if the access be too direct, it is a serious error.'

CHIMNEY-PIECE

The chimney-piece is of mottled Penmon limestone, painted to match the ground colour of the wallpaper.

FURNITURE

The carved oak bed, dressing-table, dressing-glass, cheval glass and *tables de nuit* are all Hopper designs from the 1830s. Other pieces share the Eastern exoticism of the wallpaper: two Japanese black and gilt lacquer cabinets*, the one eighteenth-century on an ebonised stand in the style of William Kent, and the other seventeenth-century on a much later plain

The Lower India Room

ebonised stand*; a Chinese black and gilt lacquer tilt-top table, *c*.1810; and an unusually tall wardrobe, assembled *c*.1800 from earlier Chinese panels. The main cupboard doors of this wardrobe are late seventeenth-century, with figures of horsemen applied in mother-of-pearl and various hardstones; the drawer-fronts are also seventeenth-century, but the lower doors, decorated with European figures, are eighteenth-century.

CERAMICS

ON THE MANTELPIECE:
A pair of early nineteenth-century Chinese *cloisonné* vases, and several eighteenth- and nineteenth-century Chinese blue-and-white vessels.

IN THE CORNER:
A very large blue-and-white late-nineteenth-century Chinese vase.
The white and gold china washstand set is Minton, *c*.1850.

PHOTOGRAPH

ON THE MANTELPIECE:
A portrait in a slate frame of Sir Prescott Gardner Hewett, Bt (1812–91), a family friend who became Surgeon Extraordinary to Queen Victoria, and saved the artistic career of Carl Haag (see No.234 below).

THE CHAPEL CORRIDOR

PICTURES

131 FRENCH, early seventeenth century
Portrait of a boy wearing the Saint Esprit

234 CARL HAAG (1820–1915)
Palmyra
Watercolour, signed and dated 1863
Haag regarded the 1st Lord Penrhyn as his first true patron in England. This picture and its two companions (Nos. 235 and 236) were commissioned by Lord Penrhyn after visiting the artist's studio in 1860 with his son George and being 'swept away' by his sketches of the Levant, which the latter knew at first hand. They had been introduced by Lord Penrhyn's great friend and adviser in the matter of watercolours, the distinguished surgeon Sir Prescott Hewett. Sir Prescott's surgical skill had saved Haag's thumb and his career, after an explosion caused by 'carelessly smoking his pipe whilst cleaning his powder flask'. Queen Victoria so admired two of Haag's pictures during her visit to Penrhyn that she invited the young artist to Balmoral, 'which greatly furthered his rising fame'.

The two ancient cities of Palmyra and Baalbec were rediscovered in 1751 by James Dawkins, uncle of the builder of Penrhyn, and his friend Robert Wood, who together published two influential volumes of engravings of the ruins. Haag had been sketching at Palmyra (with the romantic figure of Janet, Lady Digby) and Baalbec in October–November 1859.

235 CARL HAAG (1820–1915)
The Ruins of Baalbec
Watercolour, signed and dated 1862

236 CARL HAAG (1820–1915)
The Acropolis at Athens
Watercolour, signed [begun in December 1860]

THE CHAPEL

For about 400 years Penrhyn was served by the Chapel whose remains survive in the pleasure ground (set up there as an eyecatcher in the late eighteenth century). The encaustic tiles in the floor of the present chapel are thought to have come from the earlier building, as are the three German fourteenth-century carved wooden panels (probably altar panels) now fitted beneath the stairs from the gallery.

The Chapel in 1846; lithograph by Hawkins

The Chapel remains almost exactly as it appeared in the 1846 lithograph by Hawkins, which can be seen in the family gallery. This space is distinguished from the body of the chapel, where the male and senior female staff would congregate, by a separate entrance and the comparative luxury of a cast-iron 'Norman' stove. The junior female staff would take their places in the gallery on the north (left) side, where prayer-book ledges are built into the arches.

STAINED GLASS

The stained-glass windows are attributed to David Evans of Shrewsbury. In the gallery window, which closely resembles Evans's work at St Giles, Shrewsbury, there are two scenes: in the upper part, the *Adoration of the Magi*, and in the lower the *Nunc dimittis* episode, loosely copied from the right-hand panel of Rubens's *Descent from the Cross* triptych at Antwerp. Simeon is the central figure with an up-turned face.

THE SECONDARY STAIRCASE

In many houses this monumental construction in grey sandstone, with its great lantern above, would be considered quite good enough as a principal staircase. At Penrhyn, it is relegated to second place. It was built immediately next to the Grand Stairs, so that staff and members of the family or guests should not meet on the same stair. The upper walls were formerly hung with paintings but the light from the lantern was too strong, and in 1928 the Clarkson Stanfield (No.109, Keep), which used to hang here, was recorded as 'spoilt by the sun'.

THE GRAND HALL (AISLES)

STAINED GLASS

At close quarters, Willement's ingenuity in suggesting antiquity in the round panels of his great windows can be appreciated more clearly. He used fragments of actual medieval glass (in the blue colours, for example), and 'distressed' other areas by flicking specks of paint on to the surface to suggest the pitting caused by corrosion on the outside of old windows, a practice commonly used by the eighteenth- and nineteenth-century restorers of medieval stained glass [*Please do not touch the glass*].

FURNITURE

Beneath the windows are two massive stone tables, both designed by Hopper; the first is of slate, probably enamelled by G. E. Magnus to resemble black marble, with a zig-zag motif painted on the top slab to simulate inlaid granite. The other table is of the mottled Penmon limestone seen elsewhere in the castle.

PICTURES

134 Attributed to ISAAC SEEMAN (fl.1720–51)
Sir Samuel Pennant (1709–50)
Sir Samuel became Lord Mayor of London in 1749 and died in office. His Lord Mayor's robes and chain date this portrait and its pendant (No.133, Grand Hall).

301 HENRY TANWORTH WELLS, RA (1828–1900)
Edward Gordon Douglas-Pennant, 1st Lord Penrhyn of Llandegai (1800–86)
Signed and dated 1869
Lord Penrhyn's youngest daughter Adela records: 'The sittings were very tedious to my Father, in spite of his appreciation of the good will which had caused their infliction, and when my Mother could not accompany him he used often to take me with him, although I was only a child, to Mr Wells' studio to help to while away the time.' Presented by subscription to the Town Hall, Caernarfon, and subsequently given to the National Trust.

THE DINING ROOM

Apart from the corridors, the rooms so far described offer little flat wall space for the hanging of pictures, and the two dining-rooms were clearly designed to make up for this. It is therefore puzzling that Dawkins-Pennant seems to have bought so few pictures himself (see Chapter Five), especially as a letter he received from Hopper in October 1834 hints at the possibility that the Dining Room was conceived in the knowledge of the Waterloo Gallery at Apsley House, set up in 1828–9 by Benjamin Dean Wyatt to display perhaps the most famous Old Master collection of the time. However, the Old Masters now shown here did not begin to arrive until the 1850s.

In the ceiling, the standard repertoire of Norman motifs may have been enriched by the study of West Indian botanical forms. The twenty principal leaf-bosses are encircled by bands of figurative mouldings derived from the south arch of the Norman church of Kilpeck, Herefordshire. The smaller bosses in rows dividing the larger compartments were originally much more numerous.

The use of stencilled decoration on walls and ceilings is not unusual at this date, but its extent here, covering the entire wall area above the dado, is apparently without parallel. It was an ingenious way of providing 'Norman' decoration on a flat surface; indeed, with its subtle *trompe l'oeil* shading it looks almost as if scissors and paste would transform it into a three-dimensional object. On 10 July 1834 Francis Mitchell signed an agreement to paint the Dining Room decoration for £130 following a sketch possibly by Willement. At some point in the first quarter of this century, when presumably it had become unfashionable, the stencilling was painted over, and only revealed once again in 1974.

The massive statuary chimney-piece is carved from highly polished black Penmon limestone. The supporting figures are loosely derived from the famous antique Roman figures now in the Museo Nazionale at Naples and known as the 'Farnese captives' or 'Captive barbarians', a rare classical source for the decoration at Penrhyn.

The carved wooden decoration reaches new heights of elaboration in the dado of this room, which also has a useful purpose; even in a house as 'up-to-date' as Penrhyn, it was still a very long way from the Dining Room to the 'necessary offices', and at one end of the dado on the window wall a 'secret' cupboard was fitted to accommodate Burleighware chamberpots, presumably for use only after the ladies and staff had withdrawn.

The carved wooded dado conceals a cupboard used to hold a chamberpot for the relief of gentlemen diners

PICTURES

3 AERT VAN DER NEER (1603/4–77)
Moonlight Landscape
Bought by the 1st Lord Penrhyn.

8 SALOMON KONINCK (1609–56)
A Miser
Bought by the 1st Lord Penrhyn.

23 AERT VAN DER NEER (1603/4–77)
A River Scene
Bought by the 1st Lord Penrhyn from General Phipps through the dealer Farrer for £210.

30 DAVID TENIERS THE YOUNGER (1610–90)
La Fête du Hameau (The Village Fête)
In the collection of the Empress Josephine at Malmaison by 1812. Bought by the 1st Lord Penrhyn.

38 THOMAS GAINSBOROUGH, RA (1727–88)
Wooded Landscape
Painted *c.*1775, just after Gainsborough's return to London. Bought from the Caulfield Collection, through Farrer, by the 1st Lord Penrhyn.

48 Studio of SIR PETER LELY (1618–80)
Sir John Glynne (1603–66)
Sir John Glynne was MP for Westminster in the Short and Long Parliaments. A Puritan, he became in 1655 Sergeant to the Protector and Chief Justice of the Upper Bench. The desire for self-advancement, which appears to have been his most striking characteristic, left no room for scruples; he ended his life with a knighthood and the post of King's Ancient Sergeant. When he was trampled by his horse in Charles II's Coronation parade in 1661, Pepys noted that 'people do please themselves to see how just God is to punish the rogue'. His daughter, Frances, married Sir Robert Williams, 2nd Bt of Penrhyn. The second wife of the 2nd Lord Penrhyn, Jessy Glynne of Hawarden, was also a descendant.

53 MELCHIOR DE HONDECOETER (1636–95)
Fowls and Geese
Signed
Acquired by the 1st Lord Penrhyn.

54 ANTONIO DE PEREDA (1608–78)
Two figures and a table with kitchen utensils
The picture has been enlarged at the top by the addition of a strip of canvas, 10 in. high. In the collection of Spanish pictures given to King Louis-Philippe by Frank Hall Standish; bought by the 1st Lord Penrhyn soon after the sale of Louis-Philippe's collection in 1853.

56 ALLAN RAMSAY (1713–84)
William Colyear, Viscount Milsington, later 3rd Earl of Portmore (1745–1823)
Lord Milsington's sister, Lady Juliana Colyear (see Nos.116, Passage from Breakfast Room, and 300), married Henry Dawkins in 1759. Lord Milsington succeeded his father to the earldom in 1785. Despite his benign expression in this portrait, he seems to have been of an irascible, even violent disposition. He quarrelled with his son, and left his property to his nephew James Dawkins (see No.300), whose younger brother George succeeded to Penrhyn.

58 HENRY THOMSON, RA (1773–1808)
Richard Pennant, Lord Penrhyn of Penrhyn, County Louth (1739–1808), and his dog, 'Crab'
Richard, son of John Pennant of Jamaica (No.133, Grand Hall) and of Bonella Hodges, married the Penrhyn heiress, Anne Susannah Warburton (No.59), in 1765. MP for Petersfield and subsequently for Liverpool, Richard Pennant was created Lord Penrhyn in the Irish peerage in 1783. See also No.230, and Chapter Two.

No.58 was painted in the 1790s, when Lord Penrhyn was building a road up the Nant Ffrancon to

The Dining Room

Capel Curig which established the Shrewsbury–Holyhead route perfected by Telford. Lord Penrhyn points to a map of the road, which indicates the distance saved by the new, more direct route. In the background is the Royal Hotel (now Plas y Brenin) which he built at Capel Curig in 1801, shown against a somewhat exaggeratedly mountainous background.

59 HENRY THOMSON, RA (1773–1843)
Anne Susannah, Lady Penrhyn (1745–1816)
Daughter of General Hugh Warburton (1695–1771) of Winnington Hall, Cheshire, Anne Susannah was joint-heiress to the Penrhyn estate through her grandmother, the daughter of Sir Robert Williams. In 1765 she married Richard Pennant, later Lord Penrhyn (see Nos.58 and 230), who leased and in 1785 eventually purchased the other half of the Penrhyn estate. She was somewhat eccentric on the subject of animals, and according to Alice Douglas-Pennant, the author of the picture catalogue of 1902, '[she] used to dress up her pet dogs in little coats and bonnets and people used to say "Look at the Miss Pennants" when she had them in the carriage.'

Anne Susannah's costume reveals the influence of French foreign affairs on English women's fashions in the early nineteenth century. Her turban *à la Turque* was inspired by the Turkish Embassy of 1802; the ubiquitous Cashmere shawl was popularised by the Egyptian Campaign of the 1790s, and proved indispensable for its warmth over the flimsy fabrics of the 1800s.

68 EDEN EDDIS (1812–1901)
Edward Gordon Douglas-Pennant, 1st Lord Penrhyn of Llandegai (1800–86)
Edward Gordon Douglas, son of the Hon. John Douglas and grandson of the 14th Earl of Morton, married first in 1833 Juliana Dawkins-Pennant, daughter of George Hay Dawkins-Pennant (Nos.73 and 300) and heiress of Penrhyn; he married second in 1846 Lady Maria Louisa Fitzroy (No.69). He took the name of Pennant by the will of his first wife's father, and was created Lord Penrhyn of Llandegai in 1866.

This portrait was painted during the winter of 1841–2, when the painter and sitter were staying at Harewood House in Yorkshire, the family home of Lord Penrhyn's mother Lady Frances Douglas. Lord Penrhyn is depicted in a doorway resembling the entrance to Penrhyn, but with the coastal landscape imaginatively rendered, presumably for compositional reasons. The portrait is described in the 1902 catalogue as 'Considered a good likeness, but the expression does not indicate sufficient strength of character'. See also Nos.85 and 301, Grand Hall, aisles.

69 EDEN EDDIS (1812–1901)
Lady Mary Louisa, Lady Penrhyn (1818–1912)
Painted in 1847
Lady Maria Louisa Fitzroy, daughter of the 5th Duke of Grafton, and second wife of Edward, 1st Lord Penrhyn (Nos.68, 85 and 301, Grand Hall, aisles). Lady Penrhyn disliked the portrait and was caught by her husband: '. . . perched up on a table, busily engaged in painting out the bright coloured scarf with some dark paint from her own little water colour paint box, as she considered the effect too gaudy'.

73 JOHN JACKSON, RA (1778–1831)
George Hay Dawkins-Pennant (1764–1840)
The sitter assumed the name of Pennant in 1808, on succeeding his cousin, Lord Penrhyn (Nos.58 and 230) to the Penrhyn estates. In c.1820, he commissioned Thomas Hopper to build the present castle. See also No.300.

85 SIR HUBERT VON HERKOMER, RA (1849–1914)
Edward Gordon Douglas-Pennant, 1st Lord Penrhyn of Llandegai (1800–86)
Painted in 1881, this portrait was thought to be a 'most unpleasing likeness' by Lord Penrhyn's family, and Herkomer was also unhappy with it. The initial sittings were conducted at Penrhyn, in the Breakfast Room, and the portrait was completed in London. Lord Penrhyn used to say that it would come to be known as 'Portrait of a miserable old man'. See also No.68.

230 GEORGE ROMNEY (1734–1802)
Richard Pennant, 1st Lord Penrhyn (1739–1808)
Lord Penrhyn had ten sittings for this portrait in 1789. It was delivered to his house in Grosvenor Square and paid for in 1793. For another portrait and a biography, see No.58.

231 BARBARA LEIGHTON, MRS ALFRED SOTHEBY
George Sholto Douglas-Pennant, 2nd Lord Penrhyn (1836–1907)
Lord Penrhyn succeeded to his father's title and estates in 1886, when difficulties in the Penrhyn quarries were building up towards the strikes of 1896–7 and 1900–3. He married first Pamela, daughter of Sir Charles Rushout, Bt, in 1860; and second, in 1875, Jessy, daughter of the Rev. Henry Glynne of Hawarden.

300 RICHARD BROMPTON (1723–83)
Henry Dawkins (1728–1814) and his Family
Painted in 1773
George Hay Dawkins (later Dawkins-Pennant, see No.73), the boy with his hand on the greyhound's head, succeeded to Penrhyn in 1808, and built the present castle. His elder brother, James, here dressed in

red, was equally fortunate, succeeding his uncle Lord Portmore (see No.56) to the Portmore estates. Their father, Henry Dawkins, commissioned this portrait for the Dining Room at Standlynch House, Wiltshire, whose portico is partly visible in the painting, with the spire of Salisbury Cathedral in the distance. After Henry Dawkins's death in 1814, Standlynch was bought by the nation as a gift to the descendants of Lord Nelson and renamed Trafalgar House. This painting used to hang opposite Gavin Hamilton's almost equally vast painting of the discovery of Palmyra by Robert Wood and Henry's elder brother, James Dawkins (on loan to the Hunterian Art Gallery, Glasgow University).

On loan from the present head of the Dawkins family, Mr John Dawkins.

FURNITURE

Three of the carved buffets (or side-tables) are made of burr or pollard oak, and the five dining-tables are veneered in the same material. The design of the buffets is so outlandish and original that no stylistic influence can be suggested, but those on the fireplace wall differ considerably and much of their design may have been invented by individual carvers. The fourth sideboard table is of carved oak and, though contemporary with the castle, it is not a Hopper design. Around the table are twenty ebony chairs with stamped velvet seats, all of the 1830s, and some of the earlier species of ebony and ebonised chairs are set around the walls.

CLOCK

The mid-eighteenth-century French 8-day striking clock in a Boulle-work case was given a new movement by Welch of Bangor in the nineteenth century.

TEXTILES

The carpet (an English 'Savonnerie') dates from the early 1830s. The plush curtains, introduced in 1997, are similar to those which would have hung here originally. The stamped pattern, called 'Fronsac' and made in France by Claremont, is created as the fabric is passed between hot pattern rollers. Similar examples from the 1840s can be seen on the dining-chairs.

SCULPTURE AND ORNAMENT

ON THE MANTELPIECE:
A pair of nineteenth-century *tazze* (shallow bowls on feet) carved in a very fine-grained polished black limestone, possibly from Ireland or mainland Europe.
A smaller pair in the same material.
A pair of polished black limestone candlesticks designed by Hopper.

ON THE BUFFETS FLANKING THE CHIMNEY-PIECE:
A pair of eighteenth-century Swedish porphyry urns.

ON SIDEBOARD AT THE SOUTH END OF THE ROOM:
A pair of Siena marble *tazze* with bronze 'dolphin' stands, *c.*1830.
A Penmon marble obelisk.

ON THE BUFFET AT THE NORTH END:
A granite figure of Osiris, Egyptian, XXVI Dynasty [650 BC], possibly acquired by the 2nd Lord Penrhyn.

METALWORK

ON THE BUFFETS ON THE FIREPLACE WALL:
The silver includes a pair of George III tureens* and covers* by Thomas Robins, 1809, and a set of Regency salt cellars by Paul Storr, 1816.

ON THE CENTRAL DINING-TABLE:
The flatware, bearing the arms of Richard Pennant, 1st Lord Penrhyn, is all by Thomas Heming, 1771–80. The racing trophies down the centre were all won by the 2nd and 3rd Barons' racehorses:

The Clifden Cup, won by the 2nd Lord Penrhyn's horse 'Vagabond' in 1869

The Clifden Cup*, 1869, in the form of a partly gilt group of Elizabeth I on a royal progress, with a relief of Burghley House on the plinth, by Elkington & Co. Won by 'Vagabond'.
The Newmarket July Cup*, 1890, a George III silver-gilt vase, 1808. Won by 'Queen of the Fairies'.
The Queen's Gold Vase*, Ascot, 1894, a silver-gilt wine cistern bearing the Royal Arms and with a relief of charioteers on one side, by Garrards. Won by 'Quaesitum'.
The Goodwood Cup*, 1898, a William IV silver-gilt vase by Emes & Barnard, 1825. Won by 'King's Messenger'.

Also on the dining-table is a pair of Louis XV style ormolu seven-branch candelabra and two from a set of large early nineteenth-century ormolu oil lamps with stands in the form of altar candlesticks.

THE BREAKFAST ROOM

When only the family was in residence and the full complement of footmen in black and gold striped waistcoats, tail-coats and gloves was not required in the large Dining Room, meals would be taken here.

This room was redecorated in 1984–5. The original oak-grained finish was restored to the 'camber beam' ceiling, which had been painted white. The interplay of materials is again heightened by the fact that the beam on the window wall is actually made of oak. The walls, which had latterly been painted in arsenic green, were clad in silk fabric woven in Suffolk and copied from a damask hung in the great gallery at the Wallace Collection in London by Lord Duveen in 1926. The curtains were also made in 1985.

CHIMNEY-PIECE

The presence of a single bearded male head in the centre of the mantelpiece, carved in the mottled grey Penmon limestone, is a mystery. There are many other hirsute heads in plaster and stone around the castle, and these may all allude to the medieval wild men or 'wodehouses', as the antiquarian Joseph Strutt called them. Hopper also deployed 'green men', with foliage issuing from the sides of their mouths, as corbels in some of the rooms at Gosford.

The asymmetry of the doorway cannot readily be explained by the building chronology, and it may be another instance of Hopper seeking to obfuscate it.

PICTURES
14 WILLEM VAN DE VELDE (1633–1707)
Shipping in a Calm
On panel. Signed and dated 166?3

Purchased Brussels, 8 April 1861, by the dealer Farrer, and subsequently sold to the 1st Lord Penrhyn.

17 PHILIPS WOUWERMANS (1619–68)
The Conversion of St Hubert
Signed and dated 1660
Presented by the artist to the Catholic Church in Haarlem, from which it was bought by L.J.Nieuwenhuys for Willem, Prince of Orange. C.J.Nieuwenhuys sold it to the future 1st Lord Penrhyn in 1855 for £600.

St Hubert (d.727) was converted to Christianity through encountering a stag with a crucifix between its antlers when he was out hunting, and became the first bishop of Liège.

18 PHILIPS WOUWERMANS
The Miseries of War

19 REMBRANDT VAN RIJN (1607–69)
Portrait of Catrina Hooghsaet (1607–85)
Signed, dated, and inscribed: *CATRINA HOOGH/SAET/OUT 50/JAER/Rembrandt.f/1657*
A powerful late portrait by Rembrandt, of a woman aged fifty. A misreading of her name has led to her being called the wife or the mother of the painter Pieter de Hooch, but she was actually the wife of the dyer Hendrick Jacobsz. Rooleeuw. He and his wife belonged to the Mennonites, a flourishing Protestant sect whose emphasis upon an individual approach to the message of the Bible seems most closely to have matched Rembrandt's own. Rembrandt never inscribed his portraits with the sitter's identity; the present inscription was put on subsequently.

Catrina Hooghsaet is dressed in the appropriate manner for the so-called 'Regent' and Merchant class in the North Netherlands in the mid-seventeenth century. Her head-dress is, however, particularly handsome and expensive. Its most striking feature is the elaborate double *hooftijsertgen* ('head-iron'), designed to draw the head-dress tightly on to the head: Protestant custom demanded that women, especially married women, covered their heads to the extent that their hair was hardly visible. Owen Feltham's *Brief Character of the Low Countries* (1652) noted an unfortunate side-effect of these head-irons: 'Their Ear-Wyers have so nipt in their Cheeks, that you would think some Faiery, to do them a mischief, had pincht them behind with Tongs…'

The painting was previously in the collection of the 1st Lord Le Despencer and in Edmund Higginson's Saltmarshe Gallery. It was bought by the 1st Lord Penrhyn *c.*1860.

32 BERNARDO BELLOTTO
View in Venice (Camp S. Stefanin)

'The Holy Family' (detail), by Palma Vecchio (No.42)

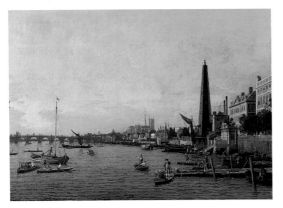

'The Thames at Westminster', Giovanni Antonio Canal (No.40)

34 SPANISH (mid-seventeenth century)
An Unknown Man
Bought as a possible Velázquez by the 1st Lord Penrhyn.

35 Attributed to ALONSO CANO (1601–67)
*An Unknown man wearing the order of Santiago**
Recent cleaning has revealed a painting of high quality which may well be an original by Cano painted not later than 1638–40, and displaying the influence of Velázquez of the 1620s and '30s. No.35 was one of the collection of Spanish pictures given to King Louis-Philippe of France by Frank Hall Standish, which was sold at Christie's in 1853 after the death of the exiled king. It was bought by the 1st Lord Penrhyn as a self-portrait by Cano. When Louis-Philippe's widowed queen and children subsequently visited Penrhyn, Lord Penrhyn tried unsuccessfully to hurry them past this picture, 'thinking the recollections it would revive would not be pleasant'.

36 After? BARTOLOMÉ ESTEBAN MURILLO (1617–82)
Don Diego Ortiz de Zúñiga (1633–80)
Copy of a lost painting probably by Murillo and once in the house of the sitter's descendants, the Marquises of Montefuerte. Ortiz de Zúñiga published a classic history of Seville in 1677. He wears the red cross of the order of Santiago, and this motif is repeated in the decorative painted frame. Bought by the 1st Lord Penrhyn from Nieuwenhuys after 1858.

40 GIOVANNI ANTONIO CANAL, called CANALETTO (1697–1768)
*The Thames at Westminster**
Canaletto was in England between 1746 and c.1755. The view shows the old York Water Gate, Pepys's former house, and the York Buildings Waterworks Company's water-tower, in the foreground, looking upriver towards Westminster Bridge. Lambeth Palace can be seen to the left of the bridge, while on the right is Westminster Hall, the old Houses of Parliament and Westminster Abbey. To the right of the Abbey, Inigo Jones's Whitehall Banqueting House can just be glimpsed between two houses on the river bank. The prominent tapering tower, which stood roughly at the bottom of the present Villiers St, housed a cistern from which the York Buildings Company supplied water to 2,500 houses.

In 1749 Sir Samuel Pennant (see No.134, Grand Hall, aisles) as Lord Mayor headed the annual water-borne cavalcade from the City to Westminster Hall, but chose Samuel Scott to record the event with just such a view of Westminster Bridge. Acquired by the 1st Lord Penrhyn from Nieuwenhuys in 1858.

42 PALMA VECCHIO (active 1510–28)
The Holy Family with SS. Jerome, Bernardino of Siena, Justina, and Ursula
St Jerome is seated to the left with his traditional attributes, the lion and a book. While preaching, St Bernardino held a tablet carved with the name of Jesus encircled by golden rays, as seen in this picture. St

'Henrietta Maria', English (No.55)

'View at Venice', Francesco Guardi (No.77)

Justina of Padua was martyred by a soldier plunging a sword into her breast as soon as she was condemned to execution. St Ursula, the legendary daughter of a British king, is shown with the flag of St George, and a model of the ship in which she sailed to her death at Cologne with 11,000 virgins. Dated to the 1520s.

Probably from the collection of King Willem II of the Netherlands; bought by the 1st Lord Penrhyn from Nieuwenhuys after 1855.

46 FRANCESCO (PACECCO) DE ROSA (1607–56)
Rebecca at the Well
Bought by the 1st Lord Penrhyn in the 1850s from Nieuwenhuys, who had imported it from Madrid as a Velázquez. Recent cleaning and restoration has fully vindicated its reattribution to this colourful Neapolitan pupil of Massimo Stanzione.

When Abraham wanted a wife for his son Isaac, to avoid his marrying one of the local Canaanite women, he sent his servant (usually called Eliezer) to find one in his original homeland, Mesopotamia. Eliezer decided to stand by a well outside Nahor and choose the first young girl to give his camels water as well as himself; this turned Out to be Abraham's great-niece, Rebecca.

51 ENGLISH (*c.*1640)
Charles I (1600–49)
Pendant to No.55.

55 ? ENGLISH (*c.*1640)
Henrietta Maria (1609–69)
Queen of Charles I. Pendant to No.51, but here the image of the queen is strongly influenced by Van Dyck, whilst the fantasy architecture seems to reflect the influence of Steenwyck the Younger, who was in London from 1617 until after 1637.

66 After ? HANS HOLBEIN (1497/8–1543)
Henry VIII (1491–1547)
On panel
This is derived from the final type of the king's portrait painted *c.*1542.

67 ENGLISH (sixteenth century)
Elizabeth I (1533–1603)
A variant of the so-called 'Ermine Portrait' of 1585 at Hatfield. It was bought by George Hay Dawkins-Pennant at Lord Charles Townshend's sale, 4 June 1819.

71 MARY BEALE (1633–99)
An Unknown Man
Signed
By family tradition, Nos.71 and 72 depict members of the Williams family of Penrhyn.

72 Manner of JOHN RILEY (1646–91)
An Unknown Lady
See No.71.

77 FRANCESCO GUARDI (1712–93)
View at Venice*
To the left the island of San Giorgio, with Palladio's church of San Giorgio. In the distance to the right, the church of the Redentore, also by Palladio. Bought by Edward, 1st Lord Penrhyn.

79 Attributed to PIETRO BUONACCORSI, called PERINO DEL VAGA (1501–47)
Holy Family with St John the Baptist
On panel
Bought by the 1st Lord Penrhyn. The picture was a great favourite of Lord Penrhyn's son, the 2nd Lord Penrhyn, because the Virgin reminded him of his first wife, Pamela Blanche Rushout (d.1869). Accordingly, when the pictures were rehung in 1901, this painting was transferred from over the large Dining Room fireplace to Lord Penrhyn's sitting-room in the Keep.

Perino del Vaga was a member of Raphael's workshop in Rome where he worked until the Sack of Rome in 1527. If this picture is by del Vaga, it would have been painted prior to his departure for Genoa.

81 RICHARD WILSON, RA (1714–82)
Italian Landscape

90 Attributed to GIOVANNI BUSI, called CARIANI (active 1509, still living 1547)
The Virgin and Child with SS. Joseph and Catherine*
On panel
The attribution to Cariani is derived from the catalogue of 1902, which states that No.90 was probably bought by George Hay Dawkins-Pennant, and that it was 'done up' in 1899.

St Catherine is denoted by one of the spiked wheels with which the Emperor Maxentius reputedly first attempted to have her martyred. They were destroyed by divine intervention, and she was ultimately beheaded.

FURNITURE AND ORNAMENTS

The oak buffet-table on the right-hand wall is another of Hopper's designs with a polished Penmon limestone top. The other, mahogany, sideboard table is similar to the one in the Dining Room, and not by Hopper. The small oak William IV dining-table is inlaid with burr walnut. It has two further leaves. Around the walls are several more of the ebony chairs seen elsewhere in the castle. The impressive armchairs with lion masks on the arms and stuffed backs either side of the chimney-piece are partly ebonised, partly ebony-veneered, and incorporate earlier (George II) legs. They were probably made up by Hopper.

The two small two-handled vases on the mantelpiece are of the same fine-grained black limestone as the *tazze* in the Dining Room, and are decorated with Egyptian hieroglyphs, possibly by the Derby Marble Works, *c*.1850. The font-shaped black marble bowl may have been designed by Hopper. The pole-screen banner is embroidered with the arms of Edward Gordon Douglas, 1st Baron Penrhyn of Llandegai, and his second wife Lady Maria Louisa Fitzroy.

CLOCK

The 14-day French bracket clock in a Boulle-work case is by Daniel Boucheret, Paris, *c*.1710.

METALWORK

The two Regency bronze Argand lamps have been converted to electricity. The base of the ormolu candelabrum on the table is probably an Italian altar candlestick, with later arms added. The pair of two-handled bronze urns after the Antique on the mantelpiece is nineteenth-century. Their design combines the form of the 'Medici Vase' with the decoration of the equally famous 'Borghese Vase'.

CERAMICS

The large punchbowl on the 'Norman' table by the window is Chinese in the Imari style, eighteenth-century.

PASSAGE FROM BREAKFAST ROOM

PICTURES

110 HENRY HAWKINS (exhibited 1822–81)
The Penrhyn Slate Quarry
Signed and dated 1832
This picture was probably painted for George Dawkins-Pennant in the year of Princess Victoria's visit to the quarry. The Princess wrote in her journal on 8 September 1832: 'It was very curious to see the men split the slate, and others cut it while others hung suspended by ropes and cut the slate; others again drove wedges into a piece of rock and in that manner would split off a block. Then little carts about a dozen at a time rolled down a railway by themselves . . .' The picture depicts the quarry from the lower side,

showing in the middle distance Talcen Mawr or 'Gibraltar rock', blown up in 1895, and evidently contains a number of portraits.

116 ? After POMPEO BATONI (1708–87)
? *Lady Juliana Dawkins* (1726–70)
Daughter of the 2nd Earl of Portmore and sister of No.56, Dining Room; she married Henry Dawkins in 1759. George Hay Dawkins-Pennant (see Nos.73 and 300, Dining Room) was their second son. Previously anonymous, this was identified by Alice Douglas-Pennant by comparison with the likeness of Lady Juliana in the Dawkins Family Group (No.300). Although it looks like a copy of a Batoni, no original is known.

THE STAFF QUARTERS

Beyond the Breakfast Room the principal rooms of the castle were divided from the domain of the servants by two oak doors, each 4 inches thick; these, and the sharp bend in the corridor, would prevent the migration of sounds and kitchen smells from one side to the other. The domestic offices occupy considerably more of the plan than the rooms they were designed to serve, but the efficiency of their layout was clearly secondary to the need for architectural consistency from the outside.

At Penrhyn, as elsewhere, the life of the servants' 'wing' was run to some extent in parallel with that of the family apartments and the principal rooms. A strict hierarchy operated, with the housekeeper at the head, and the butler, 1st lady's maid, 1st footman and 1st housemaid following in order of precedence. Joining the household at sixteen, an undermaid (there were seven housemaids in 1883) would spend almost her entire time cleaning the staffrooms, gradually learning the work of the different departments, for instance by laying the table for the housekeeper's meals. Similarly, a young footman spent time waiting on the housekeeper and other senior staff before he could take on the same duties in the Dining Room.

In 1883, at the height of the Victorian period, the establishment consisted of 23 female housemaids, kitchen and laundry staff, and 11 male household staff, with 7 in the stables. This was not a lavish complement; at around this time at Kinmel Park near St Asaph, Denbighshire, there were 68 indoor servants. On the right of the corridor is the former Butler's Pantry (not open).

In the long corridor leading off to the right, both the original set of mechanical bells and the electrical system which superseded them are still in position.

These mechanised bells were linked by wires to levers in each room, mounted on wooden bosses carved in the Norman style. Even when the battery-operated electric bells were introduced their switches were similarly housed.

THE SERVANTS' HALL

The junior staff would assemble here three times a day for meals. Since it overlooks the entrance forecourt, the windows are set high enough to prevent observation, inward or out. Located near the back door, it also served as the waiting room for tradesmen. The cast-iron cooking range is a combined open and close fire double oven.

THE HOUSEKEEPER'S ROOM

Beyond the door in the passage, this was the principal office of the household. It is now the tearoom.

Each morning, Lady Penrhyn would meet the housekeeper here, and they would decide the daily duties. The housekeeper, butler and lady's maid had their meals together here and it was also the setting for discipline and dismissals.

THE STILL ROOM

Cakes, jams, tea and coffee were prepared here, and it served as the main kitchen when the family were away. It is now the National Trust's kitchen.

THE HOUSEKEEPER'S STORE

Linen and cleaning materials were kept here in what is now the tearoom annexe. Among its original contents in 1833 were: '14lbs Best Yellow Soap, 14lbs Mottled Soap, 1lb Rotten stone (a polishing powder), 1lb putty powder [a powder of calcinated tin, for polishing glass or metal], 6yds scouring flannel, 3lbs Pot Ash, 3lbs Soda, 3 wash leathers, 1 Plate Brush, 2lbs Poland Starch, ½lb Thumb Blue [washing indigo in small lumps], 2lbs Rush Candles, 10lbs Dip Candles, 2 Blk. Lead Brushes, etc. etc'.

THE SERVANTS' BEDROOMS

The Housemaids' Tower provided the sleeping accommodation, in separate bedrooms, for the junior female staff. Strict segregation was maintained between this tower and the Footmen's Tower, at the corner of the stable block, where the junior male servants slept.

FUEL STORES AND BRUSHING ROOM

Down the stairs, between the domestic and kitchen offices, were, on the left, the Coal Vault (132 tons were consumed in 1830, shipped to Port Penrhyn as the return cargo for vessels carrying slates to the expanding industrial towns of South Wales), and the Brushing Room, furnished simply with one large table for the brushing of clothes.

OIL VAULT AND LAMP ROOM

On the other side of the passage are the Oil Vault and the Lamp Room where, through the window, you can see how the oil lamps were cleaned, filled and trimmed. Electric lighting was only introduced by the 4th Lord Penrhyn, and as late as the turn of the century, 194 lamps had to be trimmed and lit every day during winter.

CHINA ROOM

A right turn beyond the Lamp Room and then another right turn leads to the China Room where all the tableware used by the family was stored under the supervision of the Housekeeper. Entertainment on a scale enjoyed by the 1st Lord and Lady Penryhn required a vast store of dessert and dinner services. Just one of the Minton dinner services stored here included 114 dinner plates and there was also a magnificent Minton dessert service.

COOK'S SITTING ROOM

Back along the corridor to the right is the Cook's Sitting Room. The Cook was perhaps the most important member of staff, given the ambitious catering laid on for visitors to Penrhyn, and as a result is given the highest level of comfort and a £150 per year

salary. In this room he would prepare his menus and recipes, perhaps using Theodore Garrett's *Encyclopaedia of Practical Cookery* published around 1890.

THE ROYAL VISIT IN 1894

Between July 10th and 13th 1894 Penrhyn Castle experienced some of its grandest entertaining in honour of the visit of the Prince and Princess of Wales (later King Edward VII and Queen Alexandra). There was a nine-course dinner in the evening followed by an evening party for over 200 guests, which was rounded off with a supper at midnight featuring truffled quail, lobster, *foie gras* and every other available delicacy. Over the course of three days the kitchens had prepared over 1150 individual meals, including 89 separate dishes of the greatest gastronomic quality, served to each of the 35 house-guests.

PASTRY PANTRY

Through the door can be seen plates of rich desserts laid out as if waiting to be served to the Prince and Princess of Wales and other guests. These are displayed on pieces from the 1850s Minton dessert service.

THE KITCHEN

This vast kitchen is shown as it looked during preparations for one of the banquets and a few of the menus are framed and hang on the far wall. The great roasting range was operated by a rack and pinion mechanism mounted within each hob. In front a large roasting screen protected the kitchen staff from the intense heat of the fire. Once cooked the dishes were placed in the adjacent hot-cupboard ready for sending up to the Dining Room. Beneath the windows are a selection of copper cooking pots, many original Penrhyn pieces. The large dresser and cupboards lining the walls were originally made for Alnwick Castle in Northumberland.

The kitchen range

An assortment of copper pans and kettles in the Pastry Room

THE PASTRY ROOM

The long slate benches lining two of its walls were ideal for pastry-making and the square slate pastry board and slate rolling pin were made by a quarryman at Lord Penrhyn's Bethesda quarries. The flour was stored in the lidded bin and the mixing bowls are marked 'K' for kitchen.

THE SCULLERY

This was where foods were prepared prior to cooking and where the utensils were washed. In the corner are the boilers one of which was for boiling large joints of meat and for producing hot water for washing and cleaning purposes. Alongside this the wall is lined with shelves and lockers for vegetables and above is the bacon-loft.

THE LARDERS

To the north of the scullery are the larders, the Wet Larder for uncooked meats, the Dry Larder, for cooked food and the Dairy Larder which is shown as if being used for making ice cream and for moulding butter. The hygenic benefits of storing uncooked foods completely separately from cooked ones were well understood at Penrhyn and the Wet Larder even includes a large ice-box refrigerator.

Return to the passage and out into the kitchen courtyard.

THE LAUNDRY

The main laundry was set at some distance from the castle, by the kitchen garden. This, smaller laundry was for the cleaning of household items, and was another compromise on the original, more efficient plan for interconnecting wash-house, drying room and ironing room. Originally the wash-house had a solid-fuel boiling-copper but this was later replaced by a steam boiler. After passing through a box-mangle, all the linen would be dried indoors and ironed by the five laundry maids.

Around the Outer Court are ranged the Bakehouse, Brewhouse, Gun-Room, Soup Kitchen and Ice Tower, the last two being the most unusual of Penrhyn's out-offices; the purpose of the soup kitchen is not entirely clear.

THE ICE TOWER

Penrhyn is probably unique in contriving this essential country-house utility in such a prominent architectural feature. Ice would be carted from the frozen flood-meadows of the Ogwen below the castle, shovelled at ground level into the pit (23 feet deep and lined with brick, a better insulator and less retentive of damp than stone. Bundles of straw hung from the iron hooks provided further insulation.) The ice was packed in layers until the pit was full, the access door blocked with straw, and a wooden bung let into the opening at the top. Access for extraction was by means of the gantry in the upper chamber.

THE STABLE

When Samuel Wyatt came to design Richard Pennant's new castle in the 1780s, the stables were ranged in an L-shaped configuration across the west front of the house. Although one of his drawings retained this arrangement, and another proposed to extend it to the north west, even this, neater, layout would not have resolved the medieval jumble whereby the wash-house backed on to the chapel and symmetry was impossible; above all, the proximity of the stables to the new entrance front was unacceptable. All but the chapel (which was dismantled and rebuilt further away – see p.76) was done away with, and replaced by an entirely modern stable block extending north in line with the house. Samuel Wyatt was a great pioneer in finding new applications for slate and here it was used not only for the stall partitions, mangers and mounting-blocks but for the external walls, which were built of brick and faced overall with slate.

A comparison of the drawings shows that Hopper's stables were nothing more than the recladding of the same plan in Penmon limestone, with the addition of the necessary towers, all of which were put to good use. At the northern corner the Smithy occupied the ground floor, with the Gamekeeper's Room above. The stable clock, by William Platt of Stockport and dated 1793 (possibly reused from the Wyatt stables), and the Dawkins and Pennant crests were set up on the clock tower in June 1833.

THE DUNG TOWER

A third tower, with its spectacularly cantilevered bartizan, has a domed chamber at ground level for the storage of manure, which was barrowed up a sloping passage in the wall and tipped through an oculus in the dome. The gardeners would shovel the suitably rotted material from the external door; meanwhile, in the mess room above, the stable staff enjoyed the benefit of a cheap but malodorous natural heating system.

The planning of the stables, which could accommodate 36 horses, allowed a circular 'economy' begining with the granary and hayloft and progressing in an anticlockwise direction through the stalls to the Dung Tower. In 1885, when Lord Penrhyn was running a stud at Penrhyn, the staff consisted of Mr Pickard, the stud groom (who was paid almost as much as the house steward), with two 'Pad Grooms' and a pony boy. At the same time there were three coachmen. Mr Pickard died in 1897 aged 83 after 52 years' service. The coach-houses are at the southern end of the yard, and the castle's own fire engine was housed in the north-east corner.

Some of the original loose boxes are now occupied by an exhibition, *Penrhyn: its Landscape and People*. This tells the story of the great estate which supported life at the castle and explains how the National Trust now seeks to conserve it. Upstairs the former derelict Coachman's Room, Brushing Room and Granary have been repaired and converted to create space for further temporary exhibitions.

Along the east side of the yard, the arcaded covered ride has been glazed in recent years to provide accommodation for the locomotives of the Industrial Railway Museum established in 1965. The doll collection is currently closed for refurbishment. A separate guide to the Railway Museum is available in the shop.

CHAPTER SEVEN

THE GARDEN AND PLEASURE GROUND

The grounds of the castle which the visitor sees today are typical Georgian pleasure grounds, embellished with later Victorian planting and set in extensive designed parkland (not the property of the National Trust), which makes full use of the magnificent 'borrowed landscape' of Snowdonia, the Menai Strait and Great Orme's Head.

Nothing appears to remain of the gardens of the medieval house, the 'bones' of the present landscape seeming to date from the late eighteenth century and the house designed by Samuel Wyatt. Surviving accounts show that there was much planting in the early nineteenth century at the time the present castle was being built, and this has clearly done a great deal to strengthen and enrich the original landscape design. Planting of this second phase included many newly introduced exotic species which, by late Victorian times, were celebrated as among the finest specimens of their species in the British Isles. However, Penrhyn's greatest horticul-

tural glory was achieved under the head gardenership of Walter Speed from c.1860 to 1921 when the estate was famed for the unsurpassed quality of its kitchen garden produce. Speed's expertise in the production of flowers, vegetables and particularly fruit was second to none, and under his benevolent dictatorship Penrhyn was recognised as perhaps the most prestigious training school in Britain for young kitchen gardeners; the experience gained could scarcely be rivalled by royal establishments such as Windsor and was simply not available at botanical institutions such as the Royal Botanic Gardens, Kew and Edinburgh.

The earliest surviving plan of the grounds, surveyed by G. Leigh in 1768, shows the medieval house set in a landscape of small enclosures, many of them planted with trees. The approach to the house is shown striking off at right angles to the drive across an outer courtyard, through the stable block and up to the front door of the house. South of the

The swamp garden today

house is an area quartered by paths which was probably a formal garden. The rectangular area immediately north of the house, convenient for the stables and a plentiful supply of manure, is likely to have been a kitchen garden. Several other areas are described as *gardd* or garden, notably the site of the present walled garden (*Gardd Park y Moch* or Pig Park Garden) and *Gardd Bryn Dillad* (Clothes Hill Garden, perhaps a drying green), at the foot of the slope below the castle, roughly at the point along the drive from which the visitor now sees the first view of the Keep. Three orchard enclosures are shown on the east-facing slopes below the house ('*berllan*' or *perllan*). It is not known whether *Bryn Luke* (Luke's Hill) commemorates St Luke but it may be that the chapel was dedicated to him. There is no evidence of the grand formal avenues so often planted in the seventeenth and early eighteenth centuries, nor of the English landscape style which was the height of fashion when the plan was made.

The plan of 1804 by Robert Williams, a reputable land surveyor living in Bangor, shows the landscape remodelled in the English style. The new house is shown with the stable block moved to the north. We do not know who was responsible for this new landscape design but it is clear that the grounds have been remodelled at very considerable expense. Pleasure grounds have been created around the house and the old medieval chapel moved to the north west of the house as an eye-catcher, appropriate in style to the new Gothic house. An interesting system of paths or drives has been created south east of the house, extensive belts and some clumps have been planted and other areas cleared of trees to open up vistas.

The landscaping of the grounds seems to have started as early as 1780; a surviving account states 'paid William Humphrey and his partner for carrying young trees from Winnington (Cheshire) to Penrhyn being 3 Horse Loads: £2-2-0'. A sheet of notes enigmatically entitled 'Planting for Penrhyn '97' lists many of the operations one would expect for a landscape that had been some time in the making and was approaching completion; tasks listed for the year include 'fill up the woods', 'trim the tree clumps', 'thin the wood' and 'take away firs from the kitchen garden wall and plant other trees'.

A detail from G. Leigh's survey of 1768, showing the medieval house surrounded by a patchwork of small gardens and orchards

The nature of the work and the language of the sheet suggest a date of 1797 rather than 1897 and correspond with a landscape that had been developing for some twenty years. The skilful composition of this new landscape, the way views from carriage routes and from the house have been carefully composed, suggest the involvement of an experienced landscaper; William Emes (1730–1803) or his foreman, and later partner, John Webb (1754–1828) have been suggested but there remains no proof. Both worked in Wales, and Emes created the landscapes for several houses built or remodelled by Samuel Wyatt, the closest being Baron Hill on Anglesey (1776–9).

The building of the castle by George Hay Dawkins-Pennant seems to have been accompanied by an energetic new phase of planting and landscaping. A letter survives from Messrs Austin & McAslan, Nursery & Seedsmen, Glasgow, to Dawkins-Pennant hoping for his further patronage:

We hope the trees sent you in 1822 & '23 are giving satisfaction, therefore we take the liberty of sending you a list of our prices for the season which we hope you will consider very reasonable; the Oaks, Sycamores and Ash are remarkably fine but indeed they are all in general very good; if you think of planting this season, your planting orders will have the shortest attention. We are sincerely obliged for recommending us to Viscount Kirkwall who has got a large quantity from us.

Thomas Pennant described the Penrhyn demesne in 1773 as 'once beautifully embosomed with venerable oaks'. This implies that by that date the estate had lost most of its old trees. Catherine Sinclair, in her *Hill and Valley, or Wales and the Welsh* some sixty years later seems to bear this out, stating that 'Penrhyn Castle... wants nothing but well-grown wood to be perfect'. She suggests that 'the proprietor here... might with advantage try Sir Henry Steuart's plan, and "jump" a few oaks from Richmond Park or Windsor Forest, that they may reign supreme among the thriving young family of forest trees here, most of which are completely overtopped by the keep-tower.... The deficiency... however, is one which becomes less obvious every year; for, we may say of the trees here, as the late Marquis of Abercorn answered,

A detail from Robert Williams's map of 1804, showing the area around the house extensively remodelled to create a more open landscape of paths and vistas

when complimented by George III on his oaks growing so rapidly, "They have nothing else to do."' Steuart was famous for his trick of moving very large trees around his estate at Allanton in Scotland, a feat which, although well-tried in the planting of Versailles, was little practised in Britain. Sinclair writes: 'the same set of trees used always to be obligingly transplanted... and never was known in the world before such a life of activity as those unfortunate beeches led, – no sooner comfortably settled in one spot than they were danced off their feet to another.' We do not know whether Dawkins-Pennant followed Sinclair's advice but by 1856 in his *Journal of a Tour of North Wales*, Julius Rodenberg writes glowingly of the 'centuries-old oaks' of Penrhyn.

Few records remain of the further planting of the grounds by Dawkins-Pennant and his successor, Edward Gordon Douglas-Pennant, but it is clear that both must have been enthusiastic planters, adding many exotic and newly introduced species

The swamp garden below the walled garden in 1903

to the basic framework of native species which had been established by the 1820s. The tithe map of 1841 shows the landscape near the castle little changed in outline from the map of 1804; however, a very large area north of the castle, shown as fields in 1804, has been turned into parkland generously planted with belts and clumps of trees. This new planting was clearly designed to enhance the carriage drives through this area and to provide splendid views across the Menai Strait and eastwards to Great Orme's Head, but one of the first visitors to Penrhyn in 1832, clearly somewhat impatient with the notion of a neo-medieval castle, saw things differently: 'Not a single glimpse of the country can be caught from any of the windows. The whole is closed in by trees, with the exception of a space of grass . . . But not a single flower is to be seen; because forsooth there were none around castles 500 years ago!'[1]

The new castle required changes to the landscape made for the earlier house, not least the creation of a new drive to approach the castle from the east instead of the west. The old drive was kept for some years after the building of the castle and appears in some illustrations of the then new house. To the south of the new drive it is still possible to detect the landscaping of the woodland with glades and vistas, plus a liberal scattering of the then newly introduced trees and shrubs sent back from America and China by intrepid plant hunters such as David Douglas, Robert Fortune and the brothers Lobb from the 1820s to the 1850s. Most of the exotic trees planted at this time have succumbed to old age and the fierce gales of recent years, but many were recorded in the 1880s by Angus Duncan Webster, then Head Forester. Their sizes suggest that most were planted in the late 1830s or shortly after the succession of Edward Gordon Douglas-Pennant in 1840. Although Douglas the plant hunter was not related, it is easy to imagine that Douglas-Pennant relished growing his namesake's firs: two recorded by Webster were among the oldest and finest in the country, probably planted between 1836 and 1841; the two which remain on either side of the lodge do not appear in the lithograph of 1846 but were probably planted by Douglas-Pennant shortly thereafter.

By the time of the visit of Queen Victoria in 1859 the landscape must have been approaching maturity, all the planting enhancing the magnificent views as the landscapers had intended. Victoria recorded in her diary for October 17: 'After breakfast I went out with Col. & Ly. Pennant, our children & almost all the company & planted 2 trees in Albert's & my name. Arthur [her son, the Duke of Connaught] also planted one. The day cleared & became fine & I walked with our hosts & the 3 girls in the very fine grounds. The view on the sea with Pen Man Mear [Penmaemawr] rising above it, is very beautiful.' The Queen's tree, a Wellingtonia (*Sequoiadendron giganteum*, introduced from California by William Lobb in 1835) was the first of many ceremonial plantings on the Chapel Lawn west of the castle and is one of only two remaining. Edward VII, when Prince of Wales, and his sisters Princess Maud and Princess Victoria planted trees on a visit in 1894; others were planted by the Queen of Romania, Stanley Baldwin and Anthony Eden in 1890, 1932 and 1937 respectively.

Starting his employment at Penrhyn a few years after the Queen's visit, Walter Speed reigned as Head Gardener here for 58 years under three Lords Penrhyn. He was renowned as a leading expert on the production of fruit and flowers and as a strict yet kind-hearted disciplinarian who turned Penrhyn into a centre of horticultural excellence famed throughout Britain. An obituary in the October 1921 issue of *The Garden* says of him:

As a gardener nothing that Mr Speed did but he did well. As a Grape grower he was certainly second to none. Who that had seen his old faggot of Vines, pruned in his own inimitable way, will ever forget the monster bunches he grew each year, and their perfect finish? Most of his Peaches under glass he lifted and replanted each year and fed with new loam. I have seen them grown as well, but never better. His Fig trees on walls out of doors, to see them in fruit was a sight never to be forgotten. Carnations and plants generally under glass were well done. The old-fashioned walled in flower garden near to the castle was a veritable gem when in full beauty in late summer.

Speed was one of the original recipients of horticulture's highest award, the Victoria Medal of Honour, in 1897. Penrhyn's horticultural glory

(Above) The Queen of Romania planting a Caucasian Fir (Abies nordmanniana) in the garden at Penrhyn in 1890, with Lady Penrhyn and her daughters. The ceremonial spade is shown in the Library

(Right) The top terrace of the walled garden in 1903

continued under Speed's son-in-law and successor, Mr Kneller.

Angus Duncan Webster, a Scot like the 1st Lord Penrhyn, was another particularly eminent employee of the Penrhyn estate, working as Head Forester from about 1880 until the early 1890s. His interests were not confined to trees and his many publications included several written at Penrhyn such as *British Orchids* (1886) and *Forest Flora of Carnarvonshire, More Particularly the Penrhyn Estate* (1885). His records of trees at Penrhyn give a valuable insight into the planting of the estate. Webster went on to become Chief Forester to the Duke of Bedford at Woburn Abbey in 1893 where he was remembered as the last of the 'top-hatted, tail-coated foresters' who rode round the woods in the mornings and were driven round in a gig in the afternoons. He became Superintendent of Regent's Park in 1896, a post which he held until 1920 when he emigrated to the United States.

We are fortunate in having the reminiscences of some of Penrhyn's gardeners to shed light on the peculiarly Victorian social microcosm which survived in the country's kitchen gardens until the last war. Hubert George Scrivener came to Penrhyn as an apprentice when he was in his late teens in 1906. His diary for 1908 starts assiduously in January but peters out by the summer, when evening work or other distractions seem to have taken priority. The daily tasks of an apprentice gardener are set out along with lists of bedding and other plants. Even such a sketchy record shows clearly the accumulated expertise of the kitchen gardener and the precise attention to strict regimes that was essential to achieve satisfactory results. Tasks for January include: washing nectarine trees; putting 60 pots of beans in; starting hotbed for cucumbers; boxing geraniums; potting gladioli; starting early peach house; putting strawberries in early peach house; inserting chrysanthemum cuttings; sowing 381 pots of sweet peas; starting fig house. So for the early months of the year we are told most of the jobs required to provide the family with a constant supply of fruit, vegetables, cut flowers and pot plants. The quantity and variety of produce are impressive: almost 3,000 bedding geraniums; early sweet peas in pots and late ones planted outside in

The top terrace today

twenty varieties; some 400 indoor chrysanthemums and others outside; large quantities of begonias, stocks and China Asters. There is also a list of exactly the same sort of slightly tender shrubs and climbers that we find in the walled garden today.

But it is the memoirs of John Elias Jones and Arthur F. Brown, both at Penrhyn during the 1920s, that most vividly paint a picture of the workings of the kitchen garden and its social strata. While Mr Jones gives us well-ordered data about the running of the garden, Mr Brown tells us amusing anecdotes. Many of these centre on, if not the flouting of authority, at least the tweaking of its nose; but, for all this, there is a deep respect for 'the system' and a pride in the excellence achieved that shines through all his entertaining tales. The 'inside staff' consisted of between six and eight journeymen gardeners, one 'garden boy', and the foreman, all of whom lived in the bothy, a fairly large house adjoining the kitchen garden. Most of the journeymen slept in a large room separated by partitions, each cubicle having its own single bed, wardrobe, chest of drawers and chair. The total garden staff could rise to as many as thirty in the summer and the Head Gardener was responsible for some fifty estate staff in all.

Lord and Lady Penrhyn were only usually in residence during August for grouse shooting and from October to Christmas for pheasant shooting, but during their absence produce from the kitchen garden was sent to them, each fruit individually wrapped and bunches of grapes packed so that they arrived in pristine condition, their bloom intact.

The gardeners' day began at 7am and finished at 6pm in winter with a half-hour break for breakfast and an hour for lunch. Summer hours were longer and journeymen had also to work on Saturday and Sunday mornings. Mr Jones recalls a starting wage of 8s per week (presumably after deductions for board), Mr Brown remembering the princely sum of 22s, which even after deductions allowed the occasional Saturday night out and a flutter on the horses. Writing in 1965, John Elias Jones comments: 'Everybody had the opportunity to go through all the different departments, and although one is never finished learning in gardening, we had a methodical, strict and wonderful training, and in 5 years it would be your own fault if you were not fit to go and take on more responsibility in any other good garden. There are many men in different parts of the country today who are very grateful for the training they received at Penrhyn.'

It was during Jones' and Brown's time at Penrhyn in the late 1920s that Sybil, Lady Penrhyn altered and developed the walled flower garden. Although the walls appear to date from the building of the Wyatt house, the garden was and remains predominantly Victorian in character. Lady Penrhyn altered the beds on the terrace, replaced the conservatory there with the existing loggia, and created a water garden in the area below the lower walk. The fuchsia walk, praised in a *Country Life* article of 1903 as 'the real glory of Penrhyn' which 'would be the wonder of a county in England', ran down the path from the centre of the terrace. Although there are reports of fuchsias here during the last war, when much of the garden was turned over to growing vegetables, the walk must by then have become suppressed by the magnificent eucryphias on either side. The walk has recently been reinstated along the south-west side of the garden using *Fuchsia* 'Riccartonii' and the original ironwork.

In the 1930s and 1940s Hugh Napier, 4th Lord Penrhyn, established a rhododendron walk to the north west of the castle, which includes a very large group of *Rhododendron yunnanense* and a particularly fine form of *R. decorum*, which seems to be unique to Penrhyn. Since Penrhyn became the property of the National Trust in 1951, the garden has been maintained with a fraction of the original staff while keeping most of its original character. Severe gales have depleted the stock of exotic specimen trees, all too liable to wind-blow on the shallow soil overlying rock. However, a vigorous policy of replanting and renewal, and careful management of resources have ensured that Penrhyn can retain its nineteenth-century splendour for generations to come.

NOTES

1 Lord Hatherton of Teddesley, op. cit.

The walk down from the top terrace in 1903

CHAPTER EIGHT

THE ESTATE SINCE 1808

From Richard Pennant's firm foundations the Penrhyn Estate grew in size and influence in all its departments in the nineteenth century. By 1893 it included 72,000 acres of Caernarfonshire alone, with 618 farms and 873 cottages in the county. 3,000 men were employed at the quarry, by far the largest such concern in the world. Today, covering 3,500 acres and worked to a depth of 1,500 feet, the quarry is still the largest 'hand-made' hole in the earth's surface.

Throughout the nineteenth century the estate, and the quarry in particular, continued to be the engine for economic development in the region, stimulating the growth of both Port Penrhyn and the city of Bangor. Roads, schools, houses and cottages, churches and recreation grounds were built on estate land, and often at the landlord's expense, since the income, from quarrying at least, continued to be more than ample. Like the other great estates, it fulfilled many of the functions that were to become, after the 1888 Local Government Act, those of the county councils. After that time, parliamentary reform, agricultural depression, the growth of organised labour and the rise of local administration all combined to diminish the influence of the Penrhyn Estate and its owners.

'It is but justice to the successor of the late Lord Penrhyn to say that, along with the estate, he appears to inherit the same spirit for improvement', wrote the anonymous author of *The Cambrian Tourist* in 1828, and when Dawkins-Pennant took over the estate on the death of the Dowager Lady Penrhyn in 1816, one of his first acts was to agree with his chief rival in slate production, Thomas Assheton Smith of Vaynol, a system of common prices that would avoid the limiting effects of a price war and clear the way for further expansion. Assheton Smith's Dinorwic quarries remained a

'The Penrhyn Quarry in 1832', by Henry Hawkins (No.110, Passage from Breakfast Room)

Pentre farm in the Nant Ffrancon valley on the Penrhyn estate, which includes some of the most popular destinations for walkers and climbers in Snowdonia, especially around Tryfan and the Glyderau

close second to Penrhyn for the rest of the century, and between them they dominated the industry. The Penrhyn quarry produced 40,000 tons of slate in 1820, employing 1,000 men, and growth accelerated over the next twenty years (especially after the repeal in 1831 of Pitt's wartime slate duty), under the management of James Wyatt, thirteenth child of Benjamin, whom he succeeded as general agent in 1817.

In the course of this period, the settlement that came to be known as Bethesda, close to the quarry, expanded from the first building, in 1820, of the

Independent chapel of that name. Slate was the material of the moment. The building journals carried recommendations for its use not merely on the roofs of the ever-growing cities but for fireplaces, table tops, 'fittings-up of offices or living rooms, coffee-houses, and public houses', 'panels of doors and window shutters, shelves of every sort . . . fire proofing'.[1] New workers' housing had to be built at Moel y Ci, and improvements were needed at Port Penrhyn. In 1820 Dawkins-Pennant set up a new cast-iron bridge over the Cegin so that the tramway could pass right on to the wharf, which he extended in 1827–30.

The Jamaican estates were less prosperous during the first half of the century. The dismissal of an attorney for corruption in Lady Penrhyn's time was followed by a series of stormy seasons and low yields, and in 1833 all British slaves were emancipated. But Dawkins-Pennant's main preoccupation for most of his life at Penrhyn was the construction of his new castle, and so he entrusted the aggrandisement of the estate to his son-in-law and successor.

Soon after succeeding, in 1841 Col. Douglas-Pennant had James Wyatt issue an address, printed in English and Welsh, to all his tenants, which is remarkable in revealing how much of the land was still in cultivation as opposed to pasture. Wyatt wrote that the tenantry were on a ruinous course of exhaustive cropping, shallow ploughing, and poor husbandry of hay and pasture, and as a consequence they were able to raise less stock, which in turn yielded less manure. Large-scale improvements by the landlord were also needed. 'Col. Pennant's wish is to see his Property improved', he concluded, 'and, under a better system of husbandry, a thriving and improving class of Farmers. It is impossible, in the present advancing state of society, that he can willingly suffer his Farms to continue in their present neglected and ill-arranged condition.'[2]

Old farmhouses and buildings were rapidly replaced with new ones to the agent's own designs, and in 1847 Col. Douglas-Pennant began the enlargement of the estate by accepting the mortgage of Lord Mostyn's lands in the parishes of Ysbyty Ifan and Penmachno near Betws-y-Coed. In 1854 the mortgages were transferred, and in the following year the adjacent land of the former Vaughan

Watercolour of one of the family's Jamaican plantations, Denbigh, painted by a local artist in 1871

estate of Pant Glas was also acquired from Lord Mostyn. This was sporting as well as agricultural land, including the vast moorland expanse known as the Migneint near the source of the Conwy, and it was for sporting purposes that Col. Douglas-Pennant bought the nearby villa of Glan Conway, and Dinas, the house formerly used by Thomas Telford as a base for the building of the long inclined stretch of the Holyhead road south of Betws-y-Coed. During shooting, young ladies and married couples would stay at Glan Conway, and the young men at Dinas, from where a pony and trap would bring them to Glan Conway after breakfast. The villages of Ysbyty Ifan and Penmachno preserve many examples of the 'vernacular revival' buildings put up by the estate in the 1850s, and both parish churches were rebuilt around 1860, somewhat regrettably in the case of Penmachno.

By the early 1870s the estate stood at 41,348 acres in Caernarfonshire, 5,377 at Wicken in Northhamptonshire, 121 in Kent and 77 in Buckinghamshire, yielding £71,000 per annum. Of this rent roll, the £63,000 that came from Caernarfonshire farms was not as handsome as it seemed. 'There is not much encouragement to purchase land in Caernarvonshire whatever the nominal rent may be', wrote the 1st Lord Penrhyn to a solicitor friend in 1872. 'I find that as soon as it comes into my possession the calls on me for immediate repairs, new buildings, drainage, enclosure, churches, schools, Parsonage houses, and stipends for incompetent incumbents equal if they do not exceed the total nominal rent and the purchase money is a dead loss from a pecuniary point of view ...'[3]

The mainstay of the 1st Lord Penrhyn's income was the quarry, which in 1859 produced 120,000 tons giving a net annual income of £100,000, and the port was again extended and deepened in 1855. With 2,500 men employed, it was no longer practicable to manage the quarry as part of the estate, and when James Wyatt retired in 1860 the posts of estate agent and quarry manager became separate.

Lord Penrhyn was well thought of as a proprietor and employer. In 1912 his daughter Adela recalled his readiness to hear the grievances of quarrymen 'face to face', and to visit their homes, a practice that would be reciprocated if ever any of his employees visited London, where they were invited to call at the family's London residence. Taken to the top of St Paul's by one of the family's London staff, one quarryman reported disapprovingly to his employer that there seemed to be far too many brick tiles on the surrounding roofs.

Lord Penrhyn was dismayed when, in 1865, the quarrymen began to form themselves into a union. Concerned that his traditional paternalistic approach was being threatened by the emergence of an intermediary body, he quickly saw to its disbandment. However, in the next ten years the movement towards organisation grew, and in 1874, the year in which steam locomotives were first introduced on a new railway to the port, the North Wales Quarrymen's Union was officially formed, with the immediate support of more than half the employees in the region. After a brief strike its role was recognised at the Penrhyn quarry by the Pennant Lloyd Agreement, named after Lord Penrhyn's agent. Both Lord Penrhyn and his heir George Sholto were recovering from illness at the

time. Later, Adela Douglas-Pennant wrote that had they been fully involved a firmer line would have been taken, but 'sooner or later the wave of trades unionism surging over the land must have swept into the quarry'.

The firm line was adopted by George Sholto when he took over the quarry business in 1885, a year before succeeding as 2nd Baron. Profits had declined since 1874, which he attributed entirely to the influence of the union and their committee. He revoked the Pennant Lloyd Agreement with the words 'I decline altogether to sanction the interference of anybody (corporate or individual) between employer and employed in the working of the Quarry'.

The next decade was characterised by increasing antagonism between the Quarrymen's Committee and the management. In 1894 the Prince and Princess of Wales came to visit the National Eisteddfod at Caernarfon. They toured the quarry under the gaze of 10,000 spectators, 3,000 of them quarrymen. Lord Penrhyn addressed the Eisteddfod

The Nant Ffrancon Pass, photographed by Roger Fenton in 1857

as its president, and urged the participants, through their artistic endeavours, to 'soar far above the grovelling jealousies of ordinary life ... let the effect of its music be to promote the study of harmony between man and man ...'

Within two years came the first major strike, in 1896–7. The Penrhyn quarry had become a focus of attention from all quarters. There was an angry debate in the House of Commons, and Lloyd George made a speech at Carmarthen, denouncing Lord Penrhyn. But this dispute, settled without major concessions on the employer's part, was but the prelude to what has become a legendary episode in industrial history, the strike of 1900–3.

Growing resentment against individual contractors employed in the quarry flared up one afternoon in October 1900 when a serious riot took place on one of the galleries. Twenty-six men were prosecuted, and David Lloyd George acted in their defence in court. Six were convicted and dismissed, but on 22 November, the day the remaining twenty returned to the quarry, the entire workforce walked out, and after negotiations with Lord Penrhyn's manager, E. A. Young, broke down, went on strike. As the strike developed, the key question became the recognition of the union as an intermediary body between the managers and employees. When the quarry reopened in June 1901, 400 men returned to work, but antagonism grew between them and the majority who remained out. Their strike pay was modest, and although large contributions came in from the national press and the TUC, many were forced to seek work in the South Wales coal-mines. When their leader, W. J. Parry, was successfully sued for libel against Lord Penrhyn, his costs were met from a public appeal, and three local choirs toured Britain to raise money for the strikers. At holiday times, when those who had left returned to their families, there was often violence which necessitated the drafting of extra police and troops.

When the press and the TUC ended their support in 1903, the strike began to collapse, and in November there was a vote in favour of a return to work. The strike ended at a time of general

A Liberal cartoon on the strike of 1900–3, seen in terms of Tenniel's illustration to Humpty Dumpty's poem in Lewis Carroll's 'Through the Looking Glass'. Herbert Asquith and the bearded MP for Carnarvonshire Arfon, William Jones, encourage Lord Penrhyn to negotiate, while Lord Penrhyn's lawyer, Sir Edward Clarke, stands on the right, saying 'He wouldn't listen to me!'

VERY STIFF AND PROUD.

(WITH APOLOGIES TO SIR JOHN TENNIEL.)

SIR EDWARD CLARKE: "He wouldn't listen to me!"

They said to him, they said it plain, "Then you must take them back again!"	But he was very stiff and proud; He said, "You needn't shout so loud!"
They said it very loud and clear; They went and shouted in his ear.	And he was very proud and stiff; He said, "I'd interview them, if——"

[The vote of censure in connection with the Penrhyn labour troubles, which will probably come on in the House of Commons next Monday, will be moved by Mr. Asquith and seconded by Mr. William Jones. Whether it will have any more effect on Lord Penrhyn than Sir Edward Clarke's efforts remains to be seen.]

depression in the slate industry, and years of hardship and bitterness followed for those who did not find a place in the reduced workforce.

On the estate at large, there had been acquisitions and heavy expenditure in improvements and new buildings (a total of £175,000 between 1867 and 1892), but rents had not risen for many years, and in 1893 the rental income from 72,000 acres had declined to £21,000. But it was a golden age in one field at least. Angus Duncan Webster, the Head Forester (see Chapter Seven), kept the practice of forestry on the estate at the forefront of the profession. He introduced new commercial species, but also paid great attention to the traditional and still economically important woodland industries of charcoal, bark and coppice production.

Among Webster's duties was the planting of box, privet, yew and holly for game cover, and on the southern part of the estate Lord Penrhyn's sporting interests were entrusted to Andrew Foster, Head Keeper for 28 years, and his eight staff. Five hundred brace of grouse and 3,000 pheasants were reared annually, and Foster kept up a frequent correspondence with Lord Penrhyn, which reveals an interest in natural history shared by both men. Foster's published observations, however, resulted mainly from 'vermin' shot by the keepers – 464 ravens, 16 peregrines, 1,988 kestrels, and 738 sparrow hawks between 1874 and 1902.[4]

The end of the Great Strike in 1903 coincided with a slump in the building industry, and by the time the First World War broke out production at the quarry was half that achieved in 1898. When building surged after 1918, foreign competitors and home-produced tiles inflicted further damage. Edward Sholto, 3rd Lord Penrhyn, presided, from his main seat at Wicken, over a period of retrenchment and sales, and his son Hugh Napier, 4th Baron, disposed of Richard Pennant's Royal Hotel at Capel Curig, and all the Jamaican property by 1940.

After his death in 1949, the greater part of the estate with Penrhyn Castle passed via the Inland Revenue to the National Trust, and is still managed as over 40,000 acres of mountain and upland pasture, supporting over 60 farms.

The majority interest in the quarry was acquired by Sir Alfred McAlpine Ltd in 1964. The quarry employs nearly 400 men and women, and has an annual output of nearly 500,000 tons, including some 30,000 tons of roofing slate, about one-sixth of world production.

NOTES

1 *The Architectural Magazine*, March 1834, pp.41–2.

2 *To the Farming Tenantry of the Penrhyn Estate*, 25 September 1843.

3 Penrhyn MSS, UCNW.

4 See H. E. Forrest, *The Fauna of North Wales*, 1907.

The Penrhyn Quarry in 1957, showing the galleries cut into the hillside to extract the slate

APPENDIX
PENRHYN AND THE NORMAN REVIVAL
Tim Mowl

Although the Norman Revival had a certain aesthetic and symbolic life of its own, it was from the beginning an integral part of the broader Gothic Revival. Writing in 1823, two years after Thomas Hopper had begun Penrhyn, a fellow architect and castle-builder, Robert Lugar, defined Gothic in these words:

> this ancient style of building has been very judiciously divided into three classes or characters, viz, the Castle Gothic, the Church Gothic and the House Gothic.

By this he meant quite simply buildings with round-arched windows and doors, buildings with pointed windows, and Tudor-type buildings with square-headed windows and five-centred arches. So Lugar would certainly have described Penrhyn, with its round arches, towers and defensive baronial air, as designed in 'Castle Gothic'.

To add a further ambivalence of terms, it had been usual throughout the eighteenth century and well into the nineteenth to describe round-arched medieval structures not as 'Norman', which they usually were, but as 'Saxon', which they were not. Only when Thomas Rickman published *An Attempt to Discriminate the Styles of English Architecture from the Conquest to the Reformation* in 1817 was 'Norman' established as the proper term to describe the style current in England between 1066 and 1189. The problems of stylistic attribution was not finally solved until Rickman's paper of 1836 to the Society of Antiquaries which made a clear distinction between Saxon and Norman, but by that time Penrhyn was almost complete.

This means that, while Hopper may have had a wide, even a scholarly, knowledge of authentic Norman detail, he would have been designing, in his own mind, in 'Castle Gothic'. Hence, without any sense of incongruity, he was able to enrich the general Norman profile of his castle with references to Byzantium, to Venetian fortifications and to the French fifteenth century, uniting them all by the castle air of walls and defensive towers. Obviously, the phrase 'Round-arched medieval revival' is far too cumbrous to use as a popular descriptive term for this composite style of building, but historically it would be much more accurate than the brief but over-precise 'neo-Norman' which has become standard.

A crude but deliberate neo-Norman was the earliest of all the medieval revivals to be attempted in Britain after the Renaissance had broken the native tradition of building. While 'Survival' Gothic still lingered on in Oxford colleges, country churches and cottage vernacular, and almost a century before the accepted 'Gothick' revival of the early eighteenth century, in 1637–8 a celebrated national building, the Tower of London, was refaced and refenestrated in what has to be described as a 'Norman Response'. The name of the architect who supervised the operation is as surprising as the actual event, for it was Inigo Jones, the man who first introduced to England the pure forms of Palladian classicism. Perhaps the connection between Jones and the Norman is more natural than initially appears. As the authentic Norman of the eleventh century had been an attempt to revive Roman forms, the illusory familiarity of its round arches must have made it far more accessible to an architect of classical training than the Gothic would have been. The toy-fort White Tower was a conscious Stuart preservation of the Norman character of a revered monument in the heart of the capital. The earlier rhythm of buttresses and relieving arches was maintained and the narrow-splayed Norman windows were enlarged and emphasised, some without even the classicising detail of keystones.

The Upper Ward of that extraordinary palace-fortress which Hugh May designed at Windsor Castle was an even more impressive instance of a Stuart monarch, Charles II on this occasion, commissioning not a predictable classical structure, but a series of elevations which deliberately referred back to the original Norman foundation of the castle by William the Conqueror. Their uneasy grasp of the English sceptre may explain why at least two Stuart kings felt the need to stress the continuity of royal tradition by these neo-Norman reconstructions.

In 1671, just before Hugh May began his reconditioning of Windsor, the Board of Ordnance had strengthened the defences of the Round Tower that actually stood on the Conqueror's motte. The Board used the same deep round-arched embrasures which were a regular feature of its coastal forts, and May seems to have extemporised on these to devise the deeply splayed round-headed windows which lit his State Apartments in the Upper Ward. Though the rooms within were wholly classical in style, the windows had neither keystone nor flat architrave to their exterior elevation, so they were not classical, and the fenestration which they replaced had been Gothic. This seems to leave Norman as May's most probable intention when he designed them.

Only one small tower survives of this strange composite Windsor, but it endured for well over a century and was explicitly described as 'Saxon' as late as 1824. For the whole of the eighteenth century it must, as a favourite royal residence, have lent the royal seal of approval to unwieldy neo-Norman castellation. Sir John Vanbrugh admired Windsor for its 'Castle Air' and declared that it was 'universally Approv'd'. The idea of round-arched castles fascinated him, and the many sketches which Vanbrugh made for such buildings were to have a seminal influence later in the eighteenth century. He built one, Vanbrugh Castle, as his family home on a hill behind Greenwich (1718–21), following it up with a veritable housing estate of similar structures on the land adjacent. William Stukeley, John Carter, Paul Sandby and J. C. Buckler all left sketches and studies of these villa-castles as evidence of their hold on the imagination of the century.

It was at this time of great stylistic uncertainty, immediately following the accession of George I, that the new Lord Chancellor, Thomas Parker, Earl of Maccles-field, chose for his seat not a house in the heavy old-fashioned baroque, nor one in the elegant new wave Palladian, but a decrepit moated castle, Shirburn, on the Oxford/Buckinghamshire border. Between 1716 and 1725 he poured money into its purchase and transformed a decayed structure of the late fourteenth century into a confident round-arched castle with a round brick tower at each corner. Shirburn remains to this day a building of infinite romantic appeal. Swans sail on its wide moat and a drawbridge leads to the one square gate-tower surviving from the original medieval building. Almost all the rest is of the 1720s and originally all the fenestration was round-arched. There was a family tradition that their castle was originally founded by Earl Tanquerville, who came over with the Normans in 1066. This strongly suggests that the first Thomas Parker deliberately redesigned Shirburn in a revived Norman style.

Between 1727 and 1731 another prominent politician, the 1st Earl of Strafford, built a large round-arched gate-house keep with a walled enclosure and four guard towers at Wentworth Castle in the West Riding of Yorkshire. Unfortunately, however, for the prestige of the round-arched medieval revival, this was only a folly to lend an air of antiquity to a classical main house. The next, huge, example of the style, Enmore Castle in Somerset, was begun in 1751, by the eccentric Lord Egmont, who was his own architect. Yet Enmore had little influence in the 1750s: its creator is only remembered for his bizarre ambition to turn Newfoundland into a feudal dependency. After Egmont's death his rambling castle with its dry moat, vast cellars and rebarbative façades offered no competition to the light-hearted and fanciful structures in the pointed Gothic style which were being built all over the country in response to pattern books like those of Batty Langley and the proselytising activities of Gothic enthusiasts like Sanderson Miller and Horace Walpole. What the Norman revival needed in these middle decades of the century from 1750 to 1790 was scholarly research to explore and popularise the decorative potential of the more elaborate twelfth-century work which Hopper was to deploy with such effect at Penrhyn. For want of this scholarship the impetus of the round-arched revival was lost in England. A folly tower at Virginia Water of 1757, and a tentative experiment with round-arched windows by James Wyatt at Sandleford Priory, Berkshire, in 1780–9 hardly amount to a movement.

In Scotland, where Norman kings had never ruled, but where there was a native tradition of building compact tower-houses, matters developed very differently. In 1744 the 3rd Duke of Argyll had laid the foundations of a new castle at Inveraray in Argyllshire, which, although four-square, symmetrical and Vanbrughian in inspiration, was pointed-arched Gothic in all its fenestration and entrances. Gothic Inveraray was the training ground of the Adam brothers and when during the 1770s Robert Adam was casting about for a new architectural fashion to outpoint English rivals like James Wyatt, he seems to have recalled his early experience there. More particularly he may have remembered a brilliant but unused design which a young Board of Ordnance officer, Dugal Campbell, had prepared for the 3rd Duke. Round-arched, dazzlingly geometrical in plan and offering a variety of internal room sequences, that design was the prototype for the great chain of round-arched castles which Adam designed from Culzean, Ayrshire (begun in 1777), through Oxenfoord, Midlothian (1780–2), Dalquharran, Ayrshire (designed 1782–5) to Seton, East Lothian (completed in 1792).

These urbane yet fantastic structures cannot be described as neo-Norman, for Adam was not attempting a scholarly revival of authentic Norman castles, but exploring the spatial potential of a purer round-arched form. It was a line which could have led easily to twentieth-century modernism, but only two important castles took up Adam's style south of the border: Wyatt's Norris on the Isle of Wight (1799) and Smirke's Eastnor Castle in Herefordshire (begun in 1812). For few patrons in Regency England were interested in such a use of pure form. Architectural historians like John Carter were beginning to provide the rich Norman detail which had been so notably lacking in earlier round-arched castles. Hence, when an aristocrat as prestigious as the 11th Duke of Norfolk rebuilt Arundel between 1791 and 1815, he was able to bedizen the old courtyards of the castle with a wealth of jumbled but individually authentic Norman and Gothic detail. It was Arundel rather than the unadorned solids of Norris which satisfied the mood of the age and thus a Norman Revival was launched.

Each of Arundel's separate elevations had been symmetrical. What Thomas Hopper evolved, after some clumsy experiment at Gosford Castle in Co. Armagh, was how to arrange Norman elements asymmetrically but with a satisfying and picturesque profile. Penrhyn proves how triumphantly he succeeded, yet even here the need which Hopper felt to bring in extensive elements of much later Gothic and Renaissance design suggests that Norman castles did not respond flexibly as models for modern living units.

In the 1820s the Norman Revival had provided in Gosford and Penrhyn the largest castles in Ireland and Wales. If it had been chosen as the style to reshape Windsor for George IV, its establishment would have been secure. Instead Wyatville dressed Windsor in the Gothic of Edward III's reign and that, effectively, was the end of the neo-Norman road for domestic architecture.

BIBLIOGRAPHY

MANUSCRIPT SOURCES

The Penrhyn Castle MSS, comprising 9,000 items from 1288 to 1949, are deposited in the archive of University College, North Wales, Bangor. The papers of the Penrhyn Quarry are on deposit in the Gwynedd Record Office, Caernarfon.

EARLY DESCRIPTIONS OF PENRHYN

ANON., *The Cambrian Tourist; or Post-chaise companion through Wales*, 1828

BINGLEY, Rev. W., *A Tour round North Wales performed during the Summer of 1798*, 2 vols, 1800

BINGLEY, Rev. W., *Excursions in North Wales, 3rd edition, by his son W. R. Bingley*, 1838

COSTELLO, Louise Stuart, *The Falls, Lakes and Mountains of North Wales*, 1845

EVANS, Rev. J., *The Beauties of England and Wales*, XXIV, 1809–12

HALL, Edward Hyde, 'A Description of Caernarvonshire (1809–1811)', *Caernarvonshire Historical Society Record Series*, No. 2, 1952

LLWYD, Angharad, *A History of the Island of Mona or Anglesey*, 1833

LLWYD, Richard, '*The History of Wales', revised and corrected with 'Topographical Notices'*, 1832

PARRY, John ('Bardd Alaw'), *A Trip to North Wales made in 1839*, 1839

PENNANT, Thomas, *Tours in Wales*, 1778–81, 1st collected edn, 3 vols, 1810

PÜCKLER-MUSKAU, Prince Herman Ludwig Heinrich von, *Tour in England, Ireland and France in the years 1826–1829*, 4 vols, 1832

RODENBERG, Julius, *An Autumn in Wales* (1856), 1858, trans., and ed. W. Linnard

SINCLAIR, Catherine, *Hill and Valley, or Wales and the Welsh*, 1839 [based on a journey in June–August 1833]

WILLIAMS, William, *Observations on the Snowdon Mountains*, 1802

WILLIAMS, William, 'A Survey of the Ancient and Present state of the County of Caernarfon', by 'A Land Surveyor', 1806, *Trans. Caernarvonshire Historical Society*, XXXIII, XXXIV, XXXVI, 1972–5

GENERAL

DOUGLAS-PENNANT, Hon. Adela, *A Short Summary of the life of Edward Gordon Douglas, 1st Lord Penrhyn, compiled by his youngest daughter Adela*, 1910–12 [unpublished transcript]

DOUGLAS-PENNANT, Hon. Alice, *Catalogue of the Pictures at Penrhyn Castle and Mortimer House in 1901*, 1902

DOUGLAS PENNANT, E. H., *The Pennants of Penrhyn*, 1982

DOUGLAS PENNANT, E. H., *The Welsh Families of Penrhyn*, 1985

ELLIS-JONES, Peter, 'The Wyatts of Lime Grove, Llandegai', *Trans. Caernarvonshire Historical Society*, XLII, 1981

HAGUE, Douglas B., 'Penrhyn Castle, Caernarvon – I', *Country Life*, CXVIII, 14 July 1955

HAGUE, Douglas B., 'Penrhyn Castle', *Trans. Caernarvonshire Historical Society*, XX, 1959

HASLAM, Richard, 'Penrhyn Castle, Gwynedd – I and II', *Country Life*, CLXXXI, 29 Oct., 5 Nov. 1987

HUSSEY, Christopher, 'Penrhyn Castle, Caernarvon – II and III', *Country Life*, CXVIII, 21 and 28 July 1955; reprinted in *English Country Houses: Late Georgian*, 1958, pp. 181–92

LINDSAY, Jean, *A History of the North Wales Slate Industry*, David & Charles, 1974

LINDSAY, Jean, 'The Pennants and Jamaica, 1665–1800', I and II, *Trans. Caernarvonshire Historical Society*, 1982 and 1983

LINDSAY, Jean, *The Great Strike*, 1987

LINNARD, W., 'Angus Duncan Webster: A Scottish forester at Penrhyn Castle, North Wales', *Scottish Forestry*, 1985, pp. 265–74

MOWL, Timothy, 'The Norman Revival in British Architecture 1790–1870', PhD, Oxford Univ., 1981

SALES, John, 'Victorian grandeur revived: gardens of Penrhyn Castle, Bangor, Gwynedd', *Country Life*, 31 October 1985

WYATT, Lewis William, *A Collection of Architectural Designs . . . Executed in a Variety of Buildings upon the Estates of the Right Hon. Lord Penrhyn*, 1800–1

THE FAMILIES OF PENRHYN

Asterisk denotes portrait in the house

Ednyfed Fychan (d. 1236)

Sir Tudur ab Ednyfed Fychan (d. 1278)

Goronwy ab Ednyfed (d. 1268)

Heilyn ap Sir Tudur (fl. 1246–82)

Goronwy Fychan

Griffith ap Heilyn (d. c.1340)

Madog ap Goronwy Fychan, Lord of Penrhyn

Gwilym ap Gruffydd I (d. c.1370)

Gruffydd ap Gwilym = Generys ferch Madog
(d. 1405)

Gwilym ap Gruffydd II = (1) Morfudd, dau. of Goronwy Fychan
(d. 1431)   (2) Joan, dau. of Sir William Stanley
Builder of Penrhyn manor house   of Hooton

Robin ap Gruffydd (d. 1445)

William Griffith I, = Alice Dalton of Apethorpe,
formerly Gwilym Fychan ap Gwilym   Northants
(c. 1420–83)

Griffith ap Robin (d. 1475)

Sir William Griffith II = Joan Troutbeck, niece of Sir Thomas
(c. 1445–1506)   Stanley, 1st Earl of Derby

Gwilym ap Gruffydd (d. 1500)
Builder of Cochwillan house

Sir William Griffith III (c.1480–1531)

William Williams I,
formerly William Fychan ap William
(d. 1558)

Edward Griffith = Jane Puleston   Sir Rhys Griffith (1514–80)
(1511–40)

Pyrs Griffith (1568–1628)

William Williams II (a.k.a. William Wyn)
(d. 1557)

Jane   Catherine   Ellen

William Williams III (d. 1612)

Edmund Williams of Conway (d. 1601–2)

John Williams, Archbishop of York (1582–1650)

Henry Williams

Robert Williams of Pen-y-rallt (d. 1623–4)

Sir Griffith Williams I, 1st Bt of Penrhyn,* cr. 1661 (d. 1663)

Sir Griffith Williams II,
4th Bt (d. 1684)

Sir Hugh Williams, 5th Bt of Marle,
father of 6th and 7th Bts

Edmund Williams, ancestor of
8th to 13th Bts

Sir John Glynne* (1603–66)

Gwen Williams = Sir Walter Yonge,
(d. 1730s)   3rd Bt of Escot

Anne Williams = Thomas Warburton
(d. 1730s)   of Winnington

Sir William Yonge 4th Bt = Hon. Anne Howard

Frances = Sir Robert Williams, 2nd Bt*
Glynne   (c.1629–80)

Sir John Williams, 3rd Bt
(d. 1682)

Frances Williams = (1) Robert Lloyd of Esclusham

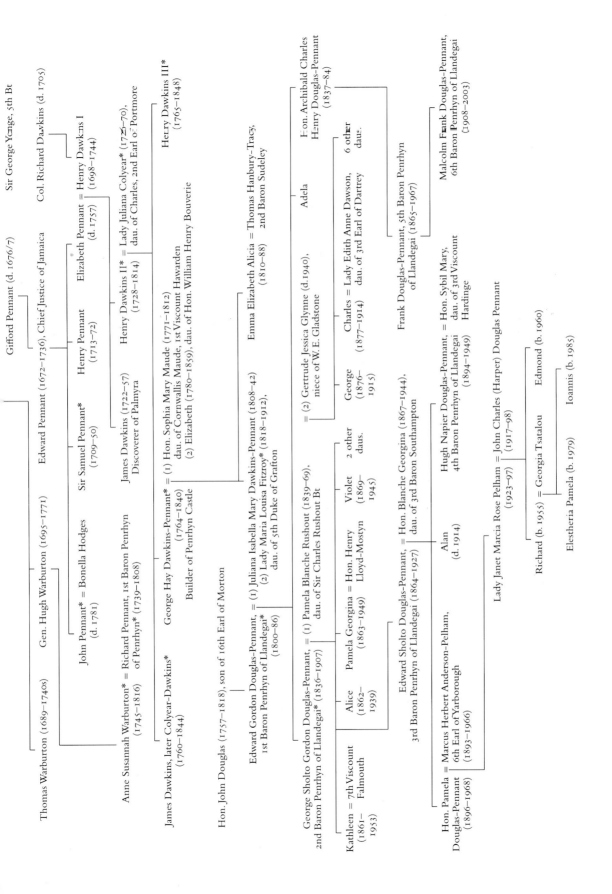

Sir George Yonge, 5th Bt

Col. Richard Dawkins (d. 1705)

Gifford Pennant (d. 1676/7)

Edward Pennant (1672–1736), Chief Justice of Jamaica

Elizabeth Pennant = Henry Dawkins I
(d. 1757)   (1698–1744)

Thomas Warburton (1689–1740s)

Gen. Hugh Warburton (1695–1771)

Henry Pennant
(1713–72)

Henry Dawkins II* = Lady Juliana Colyear* (1725–70),
(1728–1814)   dau. of Charles, 2nd Earl of Portmore

Henry Dawkins III*
(1765–1848)

John Pennant* = Bonella Hodges
(d. 1781)

Sir Samuel Pennant*
(1709–50)

James Dawkins (1722–57)
Discoverer of Palmyra

Anne Susannah Warburton* = Richard Pennant, 1st Baron Penrhyn
(1745–1816)   of Penrhyn* (1739–1808)

George Hay Dawkins-Pennant* = (1) Hon. Sophia Mary Maude (1771–1812)
(1764–1840)   dau. of Cornwallis Maude, 1st Viscount Hawarden
Builder of Penrhyn Castle   (2) Elizabeth (1780–1859), dau. of Hon. William Henry Bouverie

James Dawkins, later Colyear-Dawkins*
(1760–1844)

Emma Elizabeth Alicia = Thomas Hanbury-Tracy,
(1810–88)   2nd Baron Sudeley

Hon. Archibald Charles
Henry Douglas-Pennant
(1837–84)

Hon. John Douglas (1757–1818), son of 16th Earl of Morton

Edward Gordon Douglas-Pennant, = (1) Juliana Isabella Mary Dawkins-Pennant (1808–42)
1st Baron Penrhyn of Llandegai*   (2) Lady Maria Louisa Fitzroy* (1818–1912),
(1800–86)   dau. of 5th Duke of Grafton

Adela

= (2) Gertrude Jessica Glynne (d.1940),
niece of W. E. Gladstone

Charles = Lady Edith Anne Dawson,
(1877–1914) dau. of 3rd Earl of Dartrey

6 other
daus.

George Sholto Gordon Douglas-Pennant, = (1) Pamela Blanche Rushout (1839–69),
2nd Baron Penrhyn of Llandegai* (1836–1907)   dau. of Sir Charles Rushout Bt

George
(1876–
1915)

Frank Douglas-Pennant, 5th Baron Penrhyn
of Llandegai (1865–1907)

Malcolm Frank Douglas-Pennant,
6th Baron Penrhyn of Llandegai
(1908–2003)

Kathleen = 7th Viscount
(1861–   Falmouth
1953)

Alice
(1862–
1939)

Pamela Georgina = Hon. Henry
(1863–1949)   Lloyd-Mostyn

Violet
(1869–
1945)

2 other
daus.

Edward Sholto Douglas-Pennant, = Hon. Blanche Georgina (1867–1944),
3rd Baron Penrhyn of Llandegai (1864–1927) dau. of 3rd Baron Southampton

Alan
(d. 1914)

Hugh Napier Douglas-Pennant, = Hon. Sybil Mary,
4th Baron Penrhyn of Llandegai   dau. of 3rd Viscount
(1894–1949)   Hardinge

Hon. Pamela = Marcus Herbert Anderson-Pelham,
Douglas-Pennant 6th Earl of Yarborough
(1896–1968)   (1893–1966)

Lady Janet Marcia Rose Pelham = John Charles (Harper) Douglas Pennant
(1923–97)   (1917–98)

Richard (b. 1955) = Georgia Tsatalou

Edmond (b. 1960)

Elestheria Pamela (b. 1979)

Georgia Tsatalou

Ioannis (b. 1985)

INDEX

PLANS OF THE HOUSE

Shaded areas
not open to the public

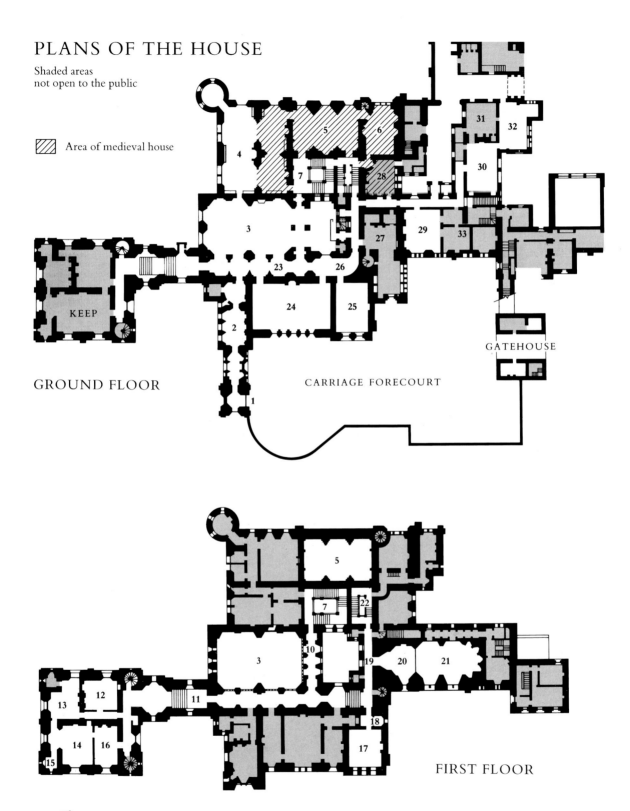

▨ Area of medieval house

GROUND FLOOR

KEEP

CARRIAGE FORECOURT

GATEHOUSE

FIRST FLOOR